Peace,
Reed Oestreich

CHRISTMAS: WHEN AND WHY

Sacred and Secular

CHRISTMAS: WHEN AND WHY

Sacred and Secular

by

Reed M. Oestreich

Illustrations by
Nelson Oestreich

BookMasters, Inc.
Mansfield, Ohio

Nelson

Sue

Lisa

Reed

Ruth

Sharing
Christmas
Memories
Around
The Tree

ACKNOWLEDGEMENTS

The author gratefully acknowledges the encouragement and help by Pastor Larry Michaels who on a Christmas tour of our home said, "Reed, why don't you write a book?"

A 'huge' thank you also goes to my daughter, Lisa Oestreich, for the many hours she spent doing all the computer work.

Thanks goes to my wife, Ruth, for giving up "the table" for weeks with piles of books and paper and with her helpful comments and encouragement.

Thank you is also in order to Madelyn Hetrick, a close friend and fellow teacher for many years at Woodmore Schools. She was so kind to do the proofreading of my book.

A special thank you goes to my brother, Nelson Oestreich. He did the original sketches in the book and also gave me encouragement and information on writing and producing a book. He is a retired art professor from Westminster College in New Wilmington, Pennsylvania.

With great appreciation I would like to thank Dan Taylor of NorthStar Design, Elmore, Ohio for the cover design and the family collage.

It has indeed been a pleasure to work with Sherry Ringler, of BookMasters, Inc., who extended encouragement and patience to me with my first book-writing endeavor.

Thanks to all for helping me make a dream come true.

An old philosopher once said, to make your life complete you must write a book, have a family, and plant a tree. I would add you also should have a firm belief in God and his son Jesus Christ.

Copyright © 1998 by Reed M. Oestreich
All rights reserved
Second Printing, 1998

Home Is Where the Heart Is

CONTENTS

Acknowledgments	vii
Preface	xv
The First Christmas	3
Advent - A Season of Preparation	10
Popular Pagan Holidays	16
December 25th ??? Christmas Day	18
Early Christianity	20
No Christmas Celebration	21
Christmas Restored	24
Interesting Facts on Christ's Birth	26
Countries - Their Own Style of Celebrating Christmas	31
- Austria	31
- France	33
- Germany	34
- Great Britain	37
- Holland	40
- Italy	43

Pre-Christmas Trees	47
Story of the History of Our Christmas Tree	50
Trimming the Christmas Tree	61
Merry Christmas - Written Round the World	87
Gift-Givers - Names Given Round the World	88
Gift-Giving Days - Days Observed Round the World	89
Nicholas - The Gift-Giver	90
The Creation of Santa Claus	93
Christmas Greens and Flowers	107
- Poinsettia	107
- Christmas Rose	110
- Mistletoe	111
- Holly	115
- Ivy	116
- Laurel	118
- Rosemary	118
The Christmas Calendar	119
The Story of *The Twelve Days of Christmas*	121
The Story of *Silent Night*	125

The Story of the Candy Cane	129
The History of the Christmas Card	132
The History of the Christmas Seal	135
The History of the Christmas Stamp	137
The Many Names for the Manger Scene	138
The Legends of The Christmas Spider	141
Music of Christmas	143
How Moravians Celebrate Christmas	147
The Moravian Star	150
Christmas Trivia	154
The Oestreich Christmas Trees	162
- Paradise Tree - Adam/Eve Tree	162
- Italian Christmas Tree - The Ceppo	164
- Friendship Tree	168
- Yum - Yum Tree	168
- Traditional - Glass Ornament Tree	169
- Wall Tree	169
- Potpourri Tree	169
- *Twelve Days of Christmas* Tree	170
- Crown Tree	170

- Early Pioneer Tree   171
- Dried - Flower Tree   172
- Goose - Feather Tree   172
- Memory Tree   175
- *For the Beauty of The Earth* Tree   175
- Spice - Herb Tree   176
- Belsnickle Tree   176
- Children's Tree   178
- The Jesse Tree   179
- German Bird Tree   181

We Bring These Gifts

PREFACE

Christmas is to be the most joyous time of the year. What is Christmas? Is it Santa Claus, gifts, Christmas trees, candles, family gatherings, church services, shepherds, wise men, Mary, Joseph, or the Baby Jesus? Probably for most of us it is a combination of all of these and much more. In Luke 2: v. 11 it says,

> "For unto you is born this day in the city of David, a Savior, which is Christ the Lord."

And in Matthew 2: v. 11 it says,

> "And when they came into the house, they saw the young child with Mary his mother, and fell down and worshipped Him."

And then Clement Clark Moore wrote,

> "Twas the Night Before Christmas and all through the house, not a creature was stirring not even a mouse..."

I truly believe that for us to enjoy and to live the Christmas season to the fullest, and to best understand Christmas, we need to search and understand the "roots" from which the season emerged. To search into the "roots" of the sacred season we need to read the Holy Scriptures and then pray for understanding. We also need to learn about the customs, habits, and general surroundings during the time of Jesus's birth. To search into the roots of the secular season we must go to the history books to

And in the sixth month
the angel Gabriel was
sent from God into
a city of Galilee,
named Nazareth
And he went into Mary
and said, Hail full of
grace, the Lord is
with thee.
And behold thou shalt
conceive in thy womb
and bring forth a son
and shalt call his
name JESUS.

And it came to pass that when Elisabeth heard the salutation of Mary, the babe leaped in her womb; and Elisabeth was filled with the Holy Spirit: And she spake out with a loud voice, and said, Blessed art thou among women, and blessed is the fruit of thy womb.

And it came to pass in those days that there went out an edict from Cesar Augustus for the registration of the whole world. And Joseph went from Galilee from the town of Nazareth into Judea unto the town of David which is called Bethlehem to be registered with Mary. And so it was, that while they were there, she brought forth her first-born son and she swathed him round and laid him in a manger, because there was no place for them in the inn.

And there was in the same district shepherds abiding in the field, keeping watch over their flocks by night. And the Angel of the Lord said unto them, Fear not; for behold, I bring you glad tidings of great joy which shall be to all people. For there has been born to you this day a Saviour who is Christ the Lord, in the town of David.

Now when Jesus was born behold there came Magi from the east to Jerusalem saying Where is he that is born King of the Jews? for we have seen his star in the east and are come to worship him. When they saw the star, they rejoiced with exceeding great joy.
And when they saw the young child with Mary his mother, they fell down and worshipped him and presented unto him gifts gold and frankincense and myrhh.

And when they were departed, behold, the angel of the Lord appeareth to Joseph in a dream, saying Arise, and take the young child and his mother and flee into Egypt, and be thou there until I bring thee word: For Herod the king will seek the young child to destroy him. When he arose, he took the young child and his mother by night and departed into Egypt.

ADVENT: A SEASON OF PREPARATION

By the fifth century, The Feast of the Nativity of the Lord Jesus Christ had become so important in the church calendar that it was considered to be the beginning of the ecclesiastical year. The start of the Church calendar was later moved back to include Advent, the season of preparation for the coming of the Christ. The Council Tours in 567 established the period of Advent as a time of fasting before Christmas and also proclaimed the twelve days from Christmas to Epiphany a sacred, festive season.

Advent comes from a Latin word "Adventus" which means "coming" or "arrival". Being a man-made period in the church calendar there are differences in its length. In the beginning Advent was a period of six Sundays modeled after the Season of Lent. Fasting - abstaining from food - was done on Mondays, Wednesdays, and Fridays. The six-week period was observed in Gaul and Northwest Italy while in Spain, Northeast Italy, and South Italy Advent was a five Sunday observance. Eventually as an edict of Rome, Advent was reduced to four Sundays. This observance has triumphed.

Some believe that Advent, emphasizing Christ's coming, should have a four-fold meaning: His coming in the flesh at Bethlehem; His coming through grace, that undeserved love through the word and sacrament; His coming at the death of each of us; and His coming in glory at Christ's second coming.

Traditionally the color of Advent, used in the church and home, was purple, the royal color of a king. Preferred in Lutheran tradition is the color blue, which had a precedent in the Swedish Church. Blue was chosen because it suggests hope, a primary theme of Advent. Other colors and combinations are used throughout the world.

Generally speaking in the liturgical church different weeks of Advent emphasize or center on different themes. The first two Sundays center on Parousia or the second coming of Jesus or as the New Testament calls it "His appearing". The third Sunday centers on John the Baptist as the herald of Christ and the fourth Sunday considers the Virgin Mary as the obedient servant chosen to bear God's Son.

In early days Advent and Lent in churches were regarded as "closed times" meaning marriages were not performed. Joyous times in the home were to be kept at a minimum. Today we tend to view Advent as a joyous time of the year because "Jesus is to be born".

When we think of Advent carols we think of *O Come, O Come, Emmanuel*. This hymn most properly belongs to the period of Advent since it celebrates the expectation of Christ's *coming* rather than His actual birth.

A wonderful custom that originated in Germany and Scandinavia is the use of the Advent calendar. This custom has now become popular in many homes in America. Sometimes the Advent calendar is the picture of a house with windows that can be opened to reveal tiny pictures. Other times it is a picture of a typical Christmas scene or snow scape that can be removed or opened, again to reveal the picture. There is one window or flap for each day of Advent, the season before Christmas, or sometimes, one for each day of December leading up to Christmas. Each day, the children are allowed to reveal one picture, word, or saying. The picture, word, or saying would thus reveal something appropriate to the season. The last and largest picture is revealed on December twenty-fifth. It is usually the nativity scene, which gives meaning to all the joy and fun that the other pictures represent.

Advent Wreath - A Preparation for His Arrival

Another popular custom of Advent is the use of the Advent wreath. The wreath is Lutheran in origin, but its sense of joyous anticipation has made it popular with many other religious groups. Many times evergreen was used as the base because Christians believed it stood for "everliving". Beginning four Sundays before Christmas, on the first Sunday of Advent, one candle is lighted. Each week a new candle is lighted as a symbol of the light that will come into the world with the birth of Jesus. On the last Sunday before Christmas, all four are lighted. Many wreathes also use one larger white candle placed in the center and burned on Christmas Day.

Many times churches will emphasize the symbolism of the four candles. One symbolism approach is: Week one - Prophecy Candle, the reminder of the foretelling of Jesus's birth by old testament prophets; Week two - Bethlehem Candle, recalling words of Micah that the Christ Child would be born in Bethlehem (Micah 5: v. 2); Week three - Shepherd's Candle, a reminder of the first people to worship the Baby Jesus; Week four - Angel's Candle, a remembrance of the angel who spoke to the Virgin Mary at the conception of Jesus and the angels who appeared to shepherds in the fields outside Bethlehem on the first Christmas.

Later in the book another Advent custom, the use of the Moravian Star will be discussed in detail.

Yes, Advent means "arrival" or "coming" of Christ. As Christians we should always be prepared for the arrival of Christ. That preparation might be in the flesh, through grace, in our personal death, or in the second coming of Christ.

O COME, O COME , EMMANUEL

O come, O come, Emmanuel,
And ransom captive Israel,
That mourns in lonely exile here
Until the Son of God appear.

Refrain
Rejoice, rejoice! Emmanuel
Shall come to you, O Israel

O come, oh come, great Lord of might,
Who to your tribes on Sinai's height
In ancient time once gave the law
In cloud, and majesty, and awe.

Refrain

Oh, come, strong branch of Jesse, free
Your own from Satan's tyranny;
From depths of hell your people save
And give them vict'ry o'er the grave

Refrain

Oh, come, blest Day-spring, come and cheer
Our spirits by your advent here;
Disperse the gloomy clouds of night,
And death's dark shadows put to flight.

Refrain

Oh, come, O Key of David, come,
And open wide our heav'nly home;
Make safe the way that leads on high
And close the path to misery.

Refrain

SATURNALIA, NATALIS SOLIS INVICTI, KALENDS: POPULAR PAGAN HOLIDAYS

Let's go back in time to the days of the early Romans. The time of the winter solstice, meaning "standing still", had always been an important season in the mythology of all peoples which, of course, would include the Romans. The sun, the giver of life, is at its lowest ebb during December. It is the shortest daylight of the year, the promise of spring is buried in cold and snow. It was at this time when the threat to human existence had to be defeated by the gods. At this time the people felt they must help the gods, through the use of magic and religious ceremonies. The people won the "war" by helping their gods and then the sun began to return in triumph. The days lengthened and spring once again returned. For all people, it was a time of great festivities.

One such celebration was held from December seventeenth to the twenty-fourth. It honored Saturnalia the god of harvest and agriculture, and was the merriest holiday of the Roman year. All businesses were closed except those that provided food or revelry. Schools closed and rich and poor gave each other gifts like candles, dolls, and holly branches. These gifts were called "Strenae". Slaves were made equal to masters. Men dressed like women or in hides of animals, caroused in the streets, and yelled "Ho Saturnalia! Ho Saturnalia". Men and women walked the streets holding candles high to encourage the sun to return to its glory and to frighten the spirits of darkness. People were allowed to gamble, which at other times of the year was against the law. Heavy drinking and feasting were encouraged. Trees were trimmed with trinkets and toys. Houses were adorned with greenery. Evergreens became a symbol of eternal life and were worshipped and studded with flowers. All the activities surrounding Saturnalia were to extol the sun's rebirth and honor Saturnus, the god of the harvest.

Another pagan celebration that was held December twenty-fifth was "Natalis Solis Invicti", a feast for the birth of the unconquered sun. Roman soldiers prayed to Mithras - a Perisan sun god - who stood for goodness, justice, and life everlasting. The people in ancient times believed that with the help from the gods the sun would conquer darkness.

The pagan celebration called "Kalends" was a New Year's celebration which lasted from January first for three days. Romans decorated their homes with lights and plants and gave gifts to their children and friends.

As centuries rolled on, the Christian era came into being. Pagan practices declined but many pagan practices existed together with significant Christian observances.

DECEMBER 25TH ??? CHRISTMAS DAY

Prior to 320 A.D. Christ's birthday was celebrated in every month of the year be it March, June, August, or November. Some scholars placed it April nineteenth while others believed it to be May twentieth, November eighteenth, and March twenty-eighth. As we know no clues can be found in the Scriptures. Early Christians gave little attention to Jesus's birth because they expected the "Second Coming" any day and in some cases viewed birthday celebrations as heathen.

In the early days of Christianity, before the fourth century, many celebrated Christ's birth on January sixth. In doing research I found two conflicting dates as to when December twenty-fifth was decreed by Pope Julius I as "The Feast of the Nativity of the Lord Jesus Christ". Many sources give 320 A.D. and 350 A.D. as the date decreed by Pope Julius I. Others say it occurred in 353 A.D. decreed by Pope Liberium. Some scholars believe that Emperor Constantine I who ruled from 312-337 and who was converted to Christianity may have instituted the Nativity Festival because he declared Christianity lawful. Prior to that time in Rome, Christians had to worship secretly for fear of punishment. As you can see there is no hard evidence that would let us know on what date Christ was born. In fact, there is no certainty even about the year. Luke does give us clues to the year by saying the angel appeared to Elizabeth " in the days of

Herod," and we know Herod died in March or April of 4 B.C. Luke also says that before Christ's birth a decree from Caesar Augustus said that all the world should be taxed and this happened when Cyrenius (Quirihius, the accepted modern spelling) was governor of Syria. Records show that the only census taking place during this time took place in 7-6 B.C. Modern scholars place the birth of Christ in approximately 6 B.C. This would be two years before the death of Herod. In my opinion it doesn't matter exactly *when* he was born, the important thing that matters is that He *was* born.

EARLY CHRISTIANITY

Around the time of 353 A.D. Rome was the center of the world. Roman armies had conquered many countries making an empire made up of many different cultures and religions. One-tenth of the people of the empire were Christians while nine-tenths were called "pagans" by the Christians.

Being concerned that the Christians might be tempted to join in the pagan festivities that occurred in December, the "Feast of the Nativity" was moved from January sixth to December twenty-fifth. This would make it easier for new believers to turn from "the worship of the *Sun* to the belief in the *Son* of God, Jesus."

In 597 Pope Gregory the Great advised that pagan customs be assimilated into the church, if the custom could be done "for the glory of God." Practices such as the use of the evergreen tree, hanging and using greenery including holly, lighting candles, having gift exchanges, and serving family feasts (dinners) were some of the pagan practices that were accepted into the Christmas customs.

NO CHRISTMAS CELEBRATION

The celebration of Christmas really seemed to have reached its height in the sixteenth and seventeenth century in England. The twelve days of Christmas were a time to indulge in unequaled revelry. Kings and bishops tried to out-do each other in entertainment, dress, tournaments, and the groaning bounty of the banquet tables. One course of such a banquet was a Christmas pie weighing 165 pounds. At one Christmas, Henry III had 600 oxen slaughtered for the King and court.

Gambling was very popular at Christmas. Edward IV actually passed an act restricting card playing to the twelve days of Christmas. By the sixteenth century, the celebration of Christmas had become a boisterous affair. Bands of mummers (men dressed like women and beasts as in the days of Saturnalia) did heavy drinking and carousing and even invaded churches disrupting services with their merriment.

Inevitably, there were reactions against what Christmas had become and against the way Christ's birthday was celebrated. There was even controversy over whether Christ's birthday should be celebrated. With the rise of some groups within Protestantism, such as the Puritans, reactions against Christmas became escalated. Some Protestant groups desired their own quieter way of celebrating Christmas in calm and meditation. The Puritans refused to celebrate at all, saying no celebration should be more important than the Sabbath.

Little change occurred until the Puritans came to power in England, beheading King Charles I and establishing Oliver Cromwell as Lord Protector of the country. Cromwell was in power thirteen years from 1647 until 1660. On June 3, 1647 punishments for celebrating Christmas were passed by parliament.

If you were living in Massachusetts in 1659 you then would be living under a similar law passed by Parliament in England in 1647. Following is a part of that statute from Massachusetts:

> "Therefore that whosoever shall be found observing any such day as Christmas, either for forbearing of labor, feasting, or any other way upon such account a foresaid, every such person so offending shall pay, for every offense, five shillings as a fine to the country."

Town criers passed through the streets ringing their bells and shouting. "No Christmas! No Christmas!" In 1681 this statue was repealed.

The Dutch settlements in New Amsterdam (later New York) continued the merriment and feasting for Christmas. Gift-giver names included: Saint Nicholas, San Claus, and Saint Nickolass.

The Town Crier - 1659

CHRISTMAS RESTORED

After the take-over by the Puritans a new form of Christmas entertainment began, that of rioting. Later in 1647 after the statute forbidding Christmas was passed, ten thousand men from Canterbury, England and the surrounding area gathered and passed their own resolution that "if they could not have their Christmas Day, they would have the king back on his throne again." Rioting and parading continued until eventually in 1660 the monarchy was restored and Christmas regained its official acceptance. This time Christmas became a celebration of the people and less an excuse for royal display. A verse became popular after the return of the monarchy of Charles I. It read:

"Now thanks to God for Charles's return,
Whose absence made old Christmas mourn;
For then we scarcely did it know,
Whether it were Christmas or no."

America took longer to recover from the Puritan influence than England. Christmas was outlawed until the middle of the nineteenth century in New England. In 1856 Christmas was still an ordinary work day in Boston and failure to report to work was grounds for dismissal. Classes were held on Christmas Day in Boston public schools as late as 1870.

Probably all the immigrants from Germany, Ireland, and other countries convinced those in power that Christmas could be a wonderful, harmless, pleasant, and even religious festivity. The first state to declare Christmas a legal holiday was Alabama in 1836. The last state was Oklahoma in 1890. By 1860 Ohio had declared Christmas a legal holiday.

Virginia colonies continued the English Christmas customs while New England condemned them. The Quakers and Puritans scorned Christmas while the Moravians, Dutch Reformed, and the Anglicans kept Christmas in their own way.

INTERESTING FACTS ON CHRIST'S BIRTH

Neither Luke or Matthew give an answer to an exact year or date of Christ's birth. Early Christians believed that the end of the world was coming soon so births were not important. Not until the sixth century did a monk named Dionysius Exiguus make calculations that became the basis for our calendar. Scholars believe the monk miscalculated and that Christ was born several years earlier than previously determined. Many believe he was born in or around 6 B.C. and in the spring time.

According to Jewish traditions Mary probably was quite young when she conceived Jesus. She was likely sixteen or younger because that was the usual time for Jewish girls to marry. Joseph probably was older since he was a craftsman and could even afford a donkey!

Jesus's birth most likely occurred in a cave that was many times used as a shelter for travelers and their beasts of burden. The swaddling cloths probably were brought along by Mary and were handmade large, soft, squares of cloth.

The manger was a feeding trough used by the animals for their hay.

The Birthplace of Jesus

Shepherds were looked down-upon, even despised. They usually were rough, ignorant, and poorly paid. Interesting enough they were the first to hear the news of Christ's birth.

Those Rough, Despised Shepherds

The wisemen were learned men and astrologers who were consulted by rulers who were making important decisions. They also were called Magi because they studied the movement of the planets and heavenly constellations. When the bright star appeared in the sky, they left their homes to find its meaning. In Matthew 2: verses 9 and 10 it reads:

> "After they had heard the King, they went on their way, and the star they had seen in the east went ahead of them until it stopped over the place where the child was. When they saw the star they were overjoyed."

There are two legends dealing with the trip of the wise men to find the Christ Child. One says they traveled for two years and that food and water never gave out. Another legend says they traveled for twelve days that seemed like one, with no need to drink or eat. That was Epiphany which is January sixth, sometimes called Three King's Day.

Typically Eastern people would have thought it rude and discourageous to pay a visit without bringing a gift. The gifts of the Wise Men were gold, frankincense, and myrrh. The gold, being very precious, symbolized Christ as King. The gift of frankincense, which was an aromatic resin used for incense, symbolized Christ as the High Priest. The myrrh, also a resin which was used for making medicine, symbolized Christ as the healer and great physician.

Worshiping the Christ Child

COUNTRIES - THEIR OWN STYLE OF CELEBRATING CHRISTMAS

To help us understand our Christmas customs, it's important that we first acquaint ourselves with those of Europe, since it is to that continent that we are most directly indebted for so much of what we do at Christmas. Austria, France, Germany, Great Britain, Holland and Italy will be discussed.

AUSTRIA

December twenty-fifth and twenty-sixth are both legal Christmas holidays in Austria. This is the most important holiday of the year. Christmas in Austria is a very musical time when carols can be heard everywhere throughout the country as Christmas approaches. This is the country that gave us in 1818 the beloved song *Silent Night ! Holy Night!*

December sixth, a day honoring the patron saint of children, is the day when Saint Nicholas and his quotesque assistant Krampus, sometimes called "the devil", make their appearance. The children must give both of them information about their good deeds and bad deeds. When the devil prepares to strike with a rod, Saint Nicholas chases the children away. When the children promise to be good, Saint Nicholas gives them nuts, fruit, and candy.

On Christmas Eve the family gathers for a family dinner. Dinner usually consists of fried or baked carp. Harper's Weekly, December 31, 1910, lists these characteristic foods: Fruchtbrod, made of raisins, currants, chopped figs and dates and made into a cake which is served hot; chopped and baked carp; beef, vegetables, and beer. After dinner the family gathers around the fir or pine tree, which is decorated with candles, cookies, and other ornaments. The presents are under the tree, but the center of attraction is the manger scene, consisting of as many as one hundred units, preserved from year to year and from generation to generation.

At midnight, Christmas services are celebrated in all Austrian Roman Catholic churches. Those walking, many times come down the mountains and through the streets with lighted torches in their hands. On December twenty-fifth and twenty-sixth families and friends visit one another and enjoy roast goose, ham, and special sweets, including rich fruit cake.

Quite wide spread are Nativity plays dealing with not only the birth of Christ, but also the stories of the shepherds and wisemen, and with the flight of the Holy Family to Egypt.

A traditional feature of Christmas Eve called "Turmblasen" is when brass instruments play chorale music from the city tower or the steeple of the church.

Another custom is "Showing the Christ Child" which consists of carrying a manger from house to house and singing carols along the way. In the mountain villages a custom prevails in which the family living farthest from the church starts with torches, caroling toward the neighbor's house.

Family after family join until they gather on the steps of the church. A final carol is sung by the whole village and they then retrace their steps to their homes.

FRANCE

The center of the home at Christmas is the crèche. "Good" children are given candy and gifts and the "bad" children are scolded or punished. There are two gift-givers: Father Christmas also named, Papa Nöelin, Pére Nöel, and Little Christmas also named, The Christ Child or le Petít Nöel.

On Christmas Eve while children are asleep toys, candies, and fruits from parents are *hung* on the tree branches. These are added to gifts from Father Christmas which are left in the shoes before the fireplace.

Christmas mass is a very important occasion taking place at midnight. After mass a big meal called reveillon is served. On Christmas morning the whole family gathers for gift exchanges. In many parts of France the adults do not exchange gifts until New Year's Day.

The Christmas tree was introduced to France but was slow to be accepted because it was introduced from Germany. It still has not gained total acceptance. When placed in the home it is decorated just a few days before Christmas.

GERMANY

Much of our modern American Christmas originated in Germany. Germany is the land of Christmas trees and Christmas toys and a place where Christmas is an important time for each person and family. Saint Nicholas' Day, December sixth, although not actually celebrated by most people marks the beginning of the Christmas season with stores, and markets presenting a festive appearance. Advent calendars, wreaths, and candles, beginning with the fourth Sunday preceding Christmas, set the mood.

Although many people have beautiful krippes (manger scenes) the Christmas tree is the center of the home with the krippe placed under it. Usually the mother does the tree trimming not allowing anyone to see the tree until six o'clock Christmas Eve.

The Christmas tree called the Tannenbaum many times uses wax candles along with gilded nuts and red apples. Also the magnificent hand-blown ornaments which have been passed down for generations are hung on the tree. Paper chains, angel hair and special cookies are also placed on the tree.

Some parts of Germany are predominately Protestant while other parts are predominately Roman Catholic. Because of this there are various customs practiced in the homes and churches.

In the sixteenth century Martin Luther declared that Saint Nicholas was robbing Christmas of its true meaning. As a result the Christ Child or

Christkindl became the gift-giver. The gifts of Christkindl are brought by a messenger, a young girl with golden hair, a golden crown, golden wings, holding a tiny "Tree of Light", and dressed in a white robe. The children were taught she traveled on the back of a white donkey, so they left a small bundle of hay for the animal to eat.

Accompanying Christkindl is a devilish character called by many names including Knecht Ruprecht, Pelznickle, Ru-klas, and Hans Trapp. These characters check on the children's behavior, threaten, and even leave bundles of rods for parents to use to discipline the children. Christkindl then banishes him from the house.

December twenty-fifth instead of December sixth (Saint Nicholas Day) became the time for receiving presents after the Reformation.

German women were wonderful cooks and bakers all year long, but especially excellent at Christmas pastries such as springerles (hard cookies with pictures stamped on them) and lebkuchens.

After the six o'clock viewing of the tree, father reads the story of the birth of Christ. Presents are then opened and Christmas Eve dinner has finally arrived. Many times the dinner consists of a feast of Karpfen (Carp), red cabbage and wonderful dessert like honey cake or stollen pastry. At this time the children sing Christmas carols.

A really special time is when the family goes to midnight service at the church. The "Big Christmas Feast" happens on early Christmas Day. But what's incredible is the real feast of Christmas is yet to come and occurs at midday. Such food as stuffed goose, plums, chestnuts, red beets, spiced cabbage and of course wine to toast the season. Then comes another round of desserts.

The Christkindl. Drawing by Thomas Nast.

GREAT BRITAIN

England probably celebrates the season with more enthusiasm, variety, and merriment than any other country. Many customs are their own and many others have made their way from all over the world. It is the land of the Yule log, the plum pudding, the boar's head, the Christmas carol, and the Christmas card. The season continues to be one of religious services, family dinners, and merry making.

The Burning of the Yule Log

Father Christmas, a non-religious gift-giver, reigns in the place of Santa Claus or Saint Nicholas. Letters are sent to him by children but are not mailed. They are thrown into the fireplace; if they go up the chimney the wish will be granted; if not one's wish goes ungranted.

During the Twelve Days of Christmas, Britain's Father Christmas went from home to home, often on a white donkey, and even on a white goat. This drawing was done in 1836 by Robert Seymour, illustrator of the Pickwick Papers in its initial serialization.

On Christmas Eve the children hang up their stockings above the fireplace or at their beds so that Father Christmas can fill them. In many homes the parents decorate the tree after the children have gone to bed. People attend midnight services on Christmas Eve and attend services again on Christmas Day. In recent years the Christmas message of the Queen is broadcast on Christmas Day.

Christmas has always been a time of feasting. Once it was English roast beef but now the dinner served in the early afternoon includes turkey, roast potatoes, mince pie, plum pudding decorated with holly and flaming brandy (called Christmas pudding) finished with candies, nuts, and fruits. In the early evening, tea would be served with a rich fruitcake covered with a thick almond-paste icing.

The Christmas tree has become a part of the festivities since Prince Albert brought it from Germany in the middle of the nineteenth century (1844). (Others say it occurred in 1841.) Greenery and mistletoe called the "kissing bough" is a real part of their decorations. The mistletoe is always hung by the oldest male member of the family.

December twenty-sixth is known as "Boxing Day". On this day boxes of food and clothing are given to those less fortunate.

HOLLAND

In Holland, Saint Nicholas Day, December sixth has remained a great day for the children even though it is predominately a Protestant country.

In America Santa appears at Thanksgiving parades; but in the Netherlands Saint Nicholas arrives on the last Saturday of November. He arrives by steamer called "Saint Nicholas Ship" and comes into the port of Amsterdam. His "double" comes into other ports and towns. During this time business and traffic stops because people pour out to the streets to greet Saint Nicholas. Groups of people act out and sing:

Look, There Is the Steamer Bringing Us Saint Nick!

> Look, there is the steamer from faraway lands.
> It brings us Saint Nicholas; he's waving his
> > hands.
> His horse is a-prancing on deck up and down.
> The banners are waving in village and town.
>
> Black Peter is laughing and tells every one,
> "The good kids get candy, the bad ones get
> > none!"
> Oh, please, dear Saint Nicholas, if Peter and
> > you would,
> Just visit our house, for we have been good.

As Saint Nicholas descends the gangplank, he is wearing a bishop's robe and miter, white gloves, and an enormous bishop's ring on his left hand. He is seated on his white horse and accompanied by Black Peter - called "the devil" - who has a sack on his shoulder, a birch rod in his hand, horns on his head, firy eyes, and a long red tongue.

They are greeted by the mayor and town officials and then lead a great parade through the streets while the church bells are ringing and the children are cheering. Participating in the parade are the police force, brass bands, Saint Nicholas and Black Peter, the mayor and dignitaries, decorated floats and groups of students.

December fifth, Saint Nicholas' Eve, is when the presents are exchanged. The presents are called "surprises" because they are disguised as much as possible to make the present more delightful. Small gifts are wrapped in large boxes or a large gift may be hidden with clues as to its location. All "surprises" must be accompanied by a bit of verse. After "surprises" are opened and enjoyed, the children are put to bed and the older people have tea and hard cookies called specilaas. Later, buttered and salted chestnuts are eaten.

Saint Nicholas and Black Peter are also involved as gift-givers. Black Peter, who was subdued by Saint Nicholas and forced to be his servant, follows carrying a bag of presents. When they arrive at a house where children live, it was Black Peter who climbed up the roof and dropped

Saint Nicholas on His White Horse

down through the chimney to deliver the presents and the birch rods. This kept Saint Nicholas from getting dirty. He puts the presents in and around the wooden shoes that the Dutch children always leave on the hearth on Saint Nicholas Eve. Then they continue on to the next house. The children of the home always would put carrots and hay in their wooden shoes for Saint Nick's white horse.

Christmas Day is celebrated in an atmosphere of serenity. There is a tree, but no presents are exchanged. Houses are decorated and special food is served but the large parties have been a part of the Saint Nicholas Eve celebrations. There are church services both Christmas Eve and morning. The afternoon is spent in the family circle with carols and story-telling and at seven a big dinner is served. December twenty-sixth, considered the "Second Christmas Day," is also considered a holiday in which it is time to relax, go out to eat, or attend a concert at a church or concert hall.

ITALY

Three weeks make up the Christmas season in Italy, from the beginning of the novena (eight days before Christmas) until after Twelfth-night after the Feast of the Nativity. During the novena, children go from place to place reciting Christmas selections and receiving coins with which they can purchase items for Christmas. In some parts of Italy men dressed like shepherds go from house to house. If they are welcomed and those visited say they are going to keep Christ in Christmas, they leave a wooden spoon to place on the front door. Later the shepherds bring their musical instruments to play and sing Christmas songs. Suprisingly the bagpipe is one of the favorite musical instruments.

Italy was the birthplace of the manger scene, which is the most important Christmas decoration. World-famous figures called "pastori" are made by craftsmen called figurari. These world-famous manger scenes are called precepios and are found in every home and church. Guests kneel and musicians sing before them. Special care is taken with the Bambino, the figure representing the baby Jesus. This figure is not put in the scene until Christmas Day and is put there by the mother of the home.

The Italians observe a very rigid fast twenty-four hours preceding Christmas Eve. Following the fast an elaborate banquet is served. The main Christmas meal varies from region to region but the Christmas Eve meal would feature roasted, baked, or fried female eel for the meatless Christmas Eve supper. Christmas dinner might consist of a capon and a variety of home-baked cakes.

Gift-giving is saved for January sixth, Epiphany not Christmas. Gifts are brought by the Christ Child. Also involved is a gift-giver called Befana, a benevolent witch, and an old woman of Palestine who foolishly refused to help the Wise Men. She brings gifts or bags of ashes for the children by coming down the chimney and filling the children's shoes. Befana always rings a bell prior to entering the chimney and always arrives on a broomstick.

The use of the evergreen Christmas tree is not a custom of Italy. Their tree is shaped like a pyramid and is called a ceppo. The ceppo is a wooden frame with several tiers of shelves. On the shelves only religiously oriented items may be placed. Examples of these would be: gold, frankincense, and myrrh; a communion set; items of nature like birds; crosses; angels; and a presepio (manger scene). The word ceppo means tree trunk and is also called the Tree of Light. The light signifies Jesus. On the end of each shelf is a candle. A sketch of a ceppo will be illustrated later in the book.

Befana - Flying Over the City
Delivering Ashes and Gifts

PRE - CHRISTMAS TREES

The custom of cutting down a whole tree and bringing it indoors is just a few hundred years old. As far as we know, only branches were brought in during pagan festivals.

One early legend says that in the tenth century, a man named Georg Jacob told a story in which all trees in the world bloomed on the night Christ was born.

There is a true story about decorated evergreen branches and trees that might explain the first Christmas trees. During the Middle Ages, German peasants and troupes of actors performed plays in front of churches on December twenty-fifth. It must be remembered that during the early years of the Christian Era most people were illiterate, unable to read the Bible and other books. The church would allow dramas or plays for moral instruction. This would be done from Advent to Resurrection. The time of Advent would be a dramatization of the creation story of Adam and Eve. The players acted out the story of how God cast Adam and Eve out of the Garden of Eden after they ate an apple from the tree of good and evil. A "Paradise Tree" also called the "Tree of Life and Knowledge" or "Christbaum" would also be displayed.

On this evergreen branch or tree-the evergreen symbolizing immortality-would be placed apples representing the fall of Adam and Eve; wafers, hosts, or small loaves of bread representing our salvation through Jesus; flowers representing life; a serpent representing the devil; and the Adam and Eve figures representing the first two human creations. In the Medieval Church December twenty-fourth was "Adam and Eve Day" leading into Christ's birthday on December twenty-fifth. People also started placing these trees in their homes.

There were two other pre-Christmas trees. One was the "pyramid," a wooden frame that held shelves with candles. It was decorated with greenery and sometimes ornaments. Gifts, food, or a manger scene could be placed on its shelves. By the early part of the twentieth century, the pyramid was almost nonexistent as a Christmas decoration outside Italy. The Italians gave the name *CEPPO* to the pyramid. The other was a "lichtstock" a flat triangle that held candles. Perhaps people thought candles would look nice on the Christbaum when they saw it next to the lichtstock and pyramid. Whatever the reason, by the 1700's Germans were decorating small indoor trees with candles.

Christbaum

Lichstock

Pyramid

49

STORY OF THE HISTORY OF OUR CHRISTMAS TREE

O CHRISTMAS TREE

O Christmas tree, O Christmas tree,
With faithful leaves unchanging;
Not only green in summer's heat,
But also winter's snow and sleet
O Christmas tree, O Christmas tree,
With faithful leaves unchanging.

O Christmas tree, O Christmas tree,
Of all the trees most lovely;
Each year, you bring to me delight
Gleaming in the Christmas night.
O Christmas tree, O Christmas tree,
Of all the trees most lovely.

O Tannenbaum, O Tannenbaum,
Wie treu sind deine Blatter!
Du grunst nicht nur zur Sommerzeit,
Nein, auch im Winter, wenn es schneit.
O Tannenbaum, O Tannenbaum,
Wie treu sind deine Blatter!

O Tannenbaum, O Tannenbaum,
Du kannst mir sehr gefallen!
Wie oft hat mich zur Weichnachtszeit

Ein Baum von dir mich hoch erfreut!
O Tannenbaum, O Tannenbaum,
Du kannst mir sehr gefallen!
>Traditional German Carol
translated by George K. Evans

The Germans have made the Christmas tree, called the Tannenbaum, a symbol of the season. Germany has countless acres of trees, so it seems that the Christmas tree linked mankind to the mysteries of the forest. Also the Germans loved the Paradise tree so much that they had it placed in their homes during the Middle Ages.

Many attempts have been made to associate the Christmas tree with the Yule tree of German and Scandinavian folklore. It was common to place an evergreen, called a Yule tree, at the entrance of a home or to plant a small specimen in a tub and bring it indoors. These green trees signified immortality and also helped people during the gloomy, dark, cold days of winter. It served the same purpose as our foliage plants which we have indoors in the winter. Although this tree was not decorated, it was loved because it was ever green.

One legend tells how Saint Boniface brought Christianity to Germany. One Christmas Eve he discovered they were going to sacrifice a young boy to the gods of their day. A giant oak was to be the scene of a sacrifice. After one stroke of Saint Boniface's ax, a wind toppled the mighty oak. The people assembled were so awed that they asked Boniface for the word of God.

Pointing to an evergreen nearby, he said that the little tree, a young child of the forest, shall be a "home tree" tonight. Boniface said it was a sign of endless life, for its branches are ever green and point toward Heaven. He said it should be the tree of the Christ Child, that it should *not* see deeds of blood, but see loving gifts and lights of kindness.

Another greatly loved story about the origin of the Christmas tree refers to Martin Luther. It is related that after walking home through the woods one Christmas Eve, he gazed up to the bright clear sky and saw the countless stars. He was so awed that when he returned home he cut a small tree, set it up for his children, and decorated it with small candles. He gathered his family around the tree to impress them with the true meaning of Christ, the Light of the World, who had so gloriously brightened the sky on that Christmas Eve.

The first reference in print to Christmas trees is a forest ordinance from Ammerschweier in Alsace, Germany in 1561. (Another source uses 1521.) The statute said that no one might cut more than one bush or tree of more than eight shoes' length for Christmas. The custom had become so popular that they felt too many trees were being taken from the forest. Nothing was mentioned as to decorations or lights.

In 1605 the first description of a decorated tree came from Strasbourg, Germany. The description said that at Christmas, fir trees would be set up in parlors and that upon the tree would be placed roses cut out of many-colored paper, apples, wafers, gold-foil, sweets, etc. It's interesting here to see the relationship to the paradise and pyramid tree in which apples, wafers, roses, and greenery were used as decorations. Probably the decorations were simply moved from one to the other.

In 1737 a writer at Wittenberg made the first reference to trees with candles.

Not everyone was impressed with the custom of Christmas trees. A professor and preacher at Strasbourg Cathedral stated the tree custom was frivolity and child's play and that children should be pointed to the spiritual cedar-tree, Jesus Christ.

In 1755 another regulation pertaining to the forests of Salzburg was made forboding the taking of small evergreen trees or bushes from the forest. People, still wanting their Christmas trees, grew trees in boxes in their yards, kept them from year to year, and brought them into their "best rooms" for Christmas Eve.

Still another account tells of Christmas trees in 1740 which were lighted and covered with gilded nuts, sheep, dolls, dishes, fruit, confectionery, and figures of the Christ Child.

The fashion of the Christmas tree seemed to have first captured the fancy of the well-to-do German people in cities and towns and then filtered down to the peasants. Part of the reason for the slow spread of popularity was that the Christmas tree was a custom cherished by the Lutherans. Thus its progress in Catholic areas was somewhat slow at first, but then became universal regardless of creed or station.

So popular was the custom that trees decked with holly, mistletoe, and little gleaming lights began to appear in cemeteries on Christmas Eve. It seems they wanted to share with the departed the brightness of the festival.

Christmas markets also called Christ Markets, sprang up in towns and cities offering toys, games, colored tissue paper, gold leaf for gilding, beads, candles, candies, and dried fruits which all could be fastened to the trees. Also stick brooms, made like a stiff brush, were sold to be used by the Pelznickles or Knecht Ruprecht to punish disobedient children.

The Christmas tree was known in England as early as 1789, though it did not become popular or generally accepted until the 1840's. At that time the ruling family, which had come from Germany had a Christmas tree at Windsor Castle. Specifically Prince Albert, Queen Victoria's consort, set up a tree in 1844 (some sources date it 1841) that later became tradition in England.

The first Christmas trees in America were probably introduced by Germans also. During the Revolutionary War, Hessians, who were German mercenaries, fought on the side of the British. These mercenaries probably set up the first American Christmas tree.

In 1747 the Moravian settlers celebrated Christmas by the use of the pyramid Christmas tree made of wood. This pyramid was brought from Germany.

From a folk culture study of the Christmas customs of the Pennsylvania Dutch Germans, we find a complete and well-documented account of the introduction of the Christmas tree. The Pennsylvania Dutch adopted many Moravian Christmas customs. The Dutch gave a prominent place to Pelznickle when he gave a pre-Christmas warning held over naughty boys and girls by saying, "Look out, or Pelznickle will catch you."

Another reference to a tree set up in a home was in Harrisburg, Pennsylvania by Reverend George Lochman, the pastor of Zion Lutheran Church.

Dr. Constantin Hering a German immigrant, set up a tree in Philadelphia in 1833 and invited patients and friends to come on certain evenings. He carried on this custom for fifty years.

Ohio had its place in the early use of the Christmas tree with reference to a family tree set up in Cincinnati, Ohio in 1835. A tree was set up by August Imgard in Wooster, Ohio in 1847.

As is true in most churches, changes are not accepted readily. That was true of Zion Lutheran Church in Cleveland, Ohio. In 1851, Rev. Henry Schwan, a 32 year old German immigrant who had been in America less than a year, decided to surprise his congregation with a decorated Christmas tree like the one in his native Hanover. He received strong condemnation by his parishioners and townspeople who looked upon the practice as being a revival of pagan customs. He did have one admirer when a child summed it up, "Mother, look -- the pastor has a tree from Heaven." Schwan saw nothing wrong since this had been done in Germany for quite a period of time. A descendant of Pastor Henry Schwan shared with me a story. Schwan decided not to put a Christmas tree in the church in 1852. A fellow Cleveland pastor named Edwin Canfield decided to have two small children deliver a tree in 1852 to Pastor Schwan for his congregation to decorate. How could the parishioners turn down and disappoint small children? So a tree was put up and this tradition has continued at Zion Lutheran Church.

Zion Lutheran Church, Cleveland, Ohio

The Christmas tree made its appearance in the White House in 1856 during the term of Franklin Pearce. Benjamin Harrison made a point to emphasize he was going to have an "old-fashioned Christmas tree."

Theodore Roosevelt, an ardent conservationist, became alarmed at the ever-increasing demand for evergreens for Christmas use. He felt so strongly that he forbade the use of a Christmas tree in the White House. He was a bit embarrassed when he learned his sons Archie and Quentin had smuggled a tree into the closet in Archie's room.

Calvin and Grace Coolidge are linked with the lighting of the first national Christmas tree. It was a gigantic spruce tree from Coolidge's native Vermont and was placed on the White House lawn in 1923. Since that time this ceremony has become a part of the Christmas observance in Washington D.C.

Franklin Roosevelt, Theodores' cousin, had different opinions about Christmas trees since he grew Norway Spruce for commercial sale at Hyde Park, his New York estate.

President Dwight Eisenhower expanded the Christmas tree ceremony by inviting twenty-seven foreign dignitaries and had a "Pageant of Peace" ceremony. Mamie Eisenhower also set a White House record when she filled the 'House' with twenty-six Christmas trees in 1959.

Evergreen trees, small or huge, have become one of the cherished symbols of Christmas. All over America this colorful and decorative object has a very special meaning. It has inspired many legends and endless numbers of stories. Now every year at Christmas millions of trees brighten our land and give glory and beauty to the greatest holiday in the modern world.

The Cherished Symbol of Christmas

Waiting for the Family

TRIMMING THE CHRISTMAS TREE

ORNAMENTS

The early German trees were fir trees whose branches were sparse and far between. The trees would be decorated with nuts, fruit, gingerbread cookies, paper roses, candies, home-made ornaments, wafers, apples and of course the pickle. Also popcorn and cranberry strings were used. Later they started attaching candles to the branches.

Then in the early 1800's the Germans in a village of Lauscha, which is nestled in the mountains of Northern Bavaria, developed a wonderful skill of glass-blowing. They would blow glass beads and also "kugels", German for round. Soon more elaborate ornaments were developed. Between 1870 - 1940 there were 5000 molds in Germany. As German immigrants came to America they started glass blowing. In Lancaster, Pennsylvania a store started a real Christmas ornament rage. That was none other than the Woolworth Store. A small number of ornaments were on the shelves and were all sold within hours. In 1890 a representative from the Woolworth Company visited Germany and ordered 1500 gross or 216,000 ornaments. They also sold quickly.

Austria, Czechoslovakia, Poland, and other countries came into the art of glass blowing. According to many experts the German ornaments are the finest yet.

If you have observed glass blowing done by hand you know it is a laborious process which brings a truly beautiful creation.

I would like to share several German legends that deal with the beautiful figure glass ornaments.

If an ornament was placed on a German tree it had to have a *meaning*.

BELLS

Bells rang throughout the world when Christ was born, according to legend. Bell ornaments symbolize the joy of the Christmas holidays.

ACCORDIONS

Accordions were the instruments of choice among the early German glassblowers. In the early 1900's there was a musical club just for accordion players. Soon the accordion became the official symbol of the glass blowers guild.

COFFEE POTS

Coffee pots are symbolic of hospitality. In Germany, as in America, it is customary to bring a gift of thanks to the host in appreciation of their invitation. Often an actual coffee pot was given to celebrate an anniversary or house warming. If not an actual coffee pot then a coffee pot ornament might be given.

BASKETS

Baskets of Christmas goodies, candies and flowers given as gifts were a means of expressing one's affection for others. Glass basket ornaments represented the Christmas spirit of selfless giving.

RABBITS

Rabbits are very shy animals with no means of protecting themselves, therefore dependent on the kindness of man. At Christmas time the rabbit represents the renewal of this faith in others to provide guidance, protection, and kindness.

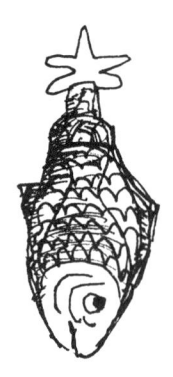

CHRISTMAS CARP

Carefully prepared during the day, this fish was often fed to family and friends on Christmas. The creation of this ornament commemorates the traditional German Christmas feast.

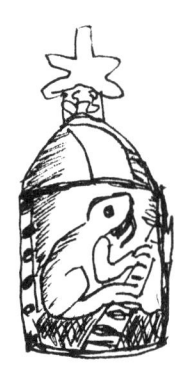

WEATHER FROGS

Weather frogs are traditional German weather forecasters. The frog provides farmers a "fool proof" means of forecasting the weather.

BIRDS

Birds are considered a symbol of happiness and are an absolute necessity on a German tree. Only a few glass-blowing families specialize in bird ornaments because they are difficult to create. Even today, birds represent messengers of love and thoughts of good things to come.

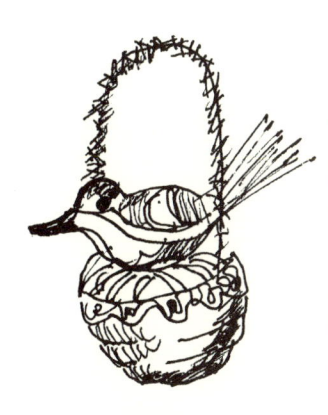

BIRD'S NESTS

These ornaments are symbols of good luck and prosperity if the nests are nestled among the branches of the tree. These should be found on every traditional German Christmas tree.

COTTAGES

These represent the heritage and culture of the glass blowers as each village has its own unique architecture of their cottages. Some are modeled after their humble homes and some after the Christmas gingerbread houses.

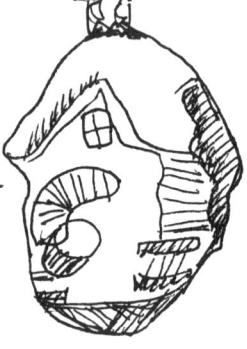

MUSHROOMS

Mushrooms are good luck symbols and are closely associated with nature and the forest Every German tree proudly displays at least one in honor of their reverence for nature. The red-headed mushroom was especially prized.

LITTLE RED RIDING HOOD

This ornament represents family values and the doctrine that children should obey their parents and remain wary of strangers. It also is on the tree to remind children of this beloved fairy tale.

LADYBUGS

The beetles received their name many years ago in Europe when aphids were attacking the grapes and the farmers prayed to the Virgin Mary for help. Soon the little red beetles appeared and ate the aphids. The farmers truly believed their prayers to Mary had been answered and so they named the beetle in honor of Mary, who was also known as "Our Lady". The beetles therefore received the name *Ladybug*.

CHIMNEY SWEEP

German folklore says that if you are touched by a chimney sweep, a professional chimney cleaner, you will have good luck and good fortune.

STARS

These ornaments originated as a symbol of guidance and faith and represent the star of Bethlehem and all stars that are at play in the Christmas traditions.

ANGELS

Angels symbolize purity, peace, and love and a comforting presence for all of us. Glass blowers often created angel faces of their own daughters.

DEVILS

The devil with red face, horns, and a tail played a real role in the early paradise plays in the Medieval times of the church. The devil head ornament is believed to be one of the earliest molds.

CLOWNS

The clowns represent the merry, jesting, nature of the German people. Following World War I the German currency lost lots of its value. Satirists said that 500,000 German marks were needed to buy a loaf of bread.

APPLES

These were the traditional Christian symbols of temptation which were hung on evergreen trees during the presentation of the paradise plays in Medieval Europe.

Also the earliest Christmas trees were adorned with natural fruits and nuts so glass blowers patterned their first molds after these items.

CARROTS

Long ago the carrot ornament was very popular in Germany as a traditional gift for brides. It was believed to bring good luck in the kitchen.

EARS OF CORN

The ears of corn ornaments have many legends that give a reminder that we should be thankful for the bountiful harvest and blessings we enjoy.

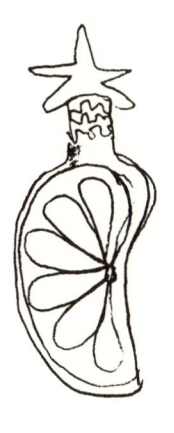

ORANGES

Oranges have always been considered a very special treat at Christmas time. Santa would often place one in the toe of the stockings of good boys and girls. Oranges were one of the earliest Christmas figure glass ornaments produced.

TOMATOES

Tomatoes long considered "love apples" were for many years thought to be poisonous by some people. In the 1840's the Germans declared the tomato edible. Because of the tomato's red and green Christmas colors, it soon became a mold for a glass ornament.

GRAPES

Grape ornaments were always considered a symbol of friendship and also symbolic of sharing a friendly glass of wine.

PICKLES

The pickle ornament was a very special German ornament that was always placed on the tree last and hidden in the branches.

When the children were allowed to see the tree, they would excitedly search for the pickle. One rule was they were not allowed to touch the tree.

One section of Germany had the custom that Saint Nicholas would leave an extra gift for the first child who found the pickle. Another section of Germany had each child come in for a certain length of time and if they found the pickle they would get a gold coin.

ACORNS

Acorns have long been considered a good luck symbol in Germany. This was because the oak trees were considered sacred. Acorns were believed to represent the rebirth of life, like the coming of the Christ Child.

CONES

Cones were again a natural decoration that were believed to be symbols of motherhood and fertility. Because of being natural they were among the first molded glass ornaments produced.

FIR TREES

Fir trees can be traced back to pre-Christmas times when they were used during the winter solstice festival called Saturnalia. Christians began using them as a reminder of Christ's gift of everlasting life.

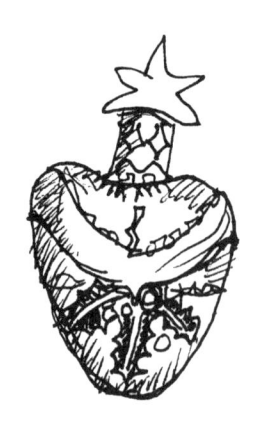

HOLLY

The holly was a symbol of life in the bleak coldness of winter. In late December, German homes would be adorned with holly to ward off evil spirits, illness, and bad winter weather. Santa Claus and Father Christmas would many times have their costumes decorated with sprigs of holly.

PANSIES

Pansies since Victorian times have been considered a sentimental flower symbolizing thoughts and feelings of love. It is said they could cure a broken heart.

TULIPS

Passion, love, and hope according to a German tradition is symbolized by the use of the tulip. It reveals true love for another person.

ROSES

Rose ornaments on a Christmas tree are believed to be an expression of love and affection. They also are symbolic of beauty.

SAINT NICHOLAS

This ornament stands for the kind, benevolent man who could perform miracles and is one of the European equivalent to the American Santa Claus.

SANTA CLAUS

This ornament stands for the jolly man in red and white who brings joy and cheer at Christmas time.

MRS. SANTA CLAUS

Mrs. Santa Claus was made because of an appeal by Americans. In Roman Catholic countries it was considered sacrilegious to have a wife for the celibate priest Saint Nicholas.

STOCKINGS

Stockings were a relatively late addition to the glass ornaments. It then was considered a rival to the Christmas tree as a gift-bearer.

NUTCRACKERS

Nutcrackers were usually dressed as soldiers and kings. A bowl of nuts was not complete without a German nutcracker standing nearby.

WALNUTS

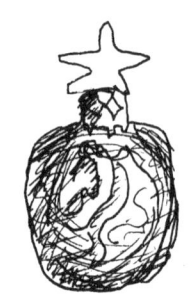

Walnuts were many times a part of early Christmas celebrations in Europe that included games and merry making. These ornaments give evidence to the brightly painted walnuts that adorned the first Christmas trees.

These glass-blown ornaments along with many, many more are used to bring joy, magic, and beauty to homes around the world.

TRIMMING

The first glass ornaments were glass chains of icicles, heavy glass balls called kugels, and glass beads. Around 1860 they reached America transported along with the treasured possessions of German immigrants. Later light-weight "chains of balls" began to appear to be used on the tree. Advertised in 1893 were: wax angels with spur-glass wings, ornaments in all conceivable shapes including hearts, acorns, birds, fruit and so on. "Glass tree points" for the top of the tree appeared along with tinsel ornaments. Silver and gilt paper and cardboard ornaments (Dresden Christmas tree ornaments) began to be sold. Cornucopias, those cone-shaped holders for nuts, candy, and fruit, began to be listed in the catalogues. Also many tin and wax ornaments were for sale.

In the December 1890 edition of *The Ladies Home Journal* an advertisement stated that cotton battings were available to simulate snow along the branches. Cotton batting under the tree also provided protection on the floor from candle wax drippings. It wasn't until 1917 that the Standard Oil Company of New York, under the trade name "Socony", put out a "dripless" candle.

The thrifty German farmers in Pennsylvania stripped Christmas trees of their needles after they had dried out and placed the skeletons in the attic. The following year the tree was covered and wrapped with cotton, so it resembled a tree in the forest after a snow storm and was then decorated. Sometimes they would return the "cotton tree" to the attic and use it over and over.

Since candles were such a fire hazard, it was a great relief when Thomas Alva Edison invented the electric light bulb in 1879. In 1895, President Grover Cleveland decorated a tree in the White House with electric lights. In 1903 electric lights on strings were invented and this invention became widely used on Christmas trees. The Ever-Ready Company of New York made these lights called "festoons" or outfits. General Electric also sold strings of twenty-eight sockets with G.E. bulbs for twelve dollars, an average man's weekly wages. In 1927 G.E. switched from an old "series" wired set to "parallel" wiring. What a blessing for not having to search for one burned out bulb!

The *Harper's Weekly* for December 28, 1867 suggested that a star placed at the top of the tree would indeed lead Santa Claus to every young child who had a decorated tree in their home.

Photographs show that around the turn of the twentieth century American Christmas trees had relatively few store-bought ornaments. Most families bought one ornament each year to add to their collection. The rest of the ornaments were still handmade.

Only one American family in five had a decorated tree in 1900. By 1930 the tree had become a nearly universal part of the American Christmas.

From the beginning of the nineteenth century, the Pennsylvania Germans decorated their trees with matzebaum, wafer-thin cakes. After slow baking at low temperatures, the matzbaums were painted with homemade vegetable dyes and many were dated and used year after year. Also baked and used were springerles and tirggels. Added were the gingerbread animal cookies and the classic gingerbread man. Popular were the cornucopias loaded with nuts, fruits, and candies.

In the mid 1860's " public trees" were social events. "Public trees" were set up in private homes, but the owner charged a small admission fee for anyone who wished to see the new novelty.

In the 1880's it was popular and fashionable among the wealthy to have "tree parties" during the holidays to amaze and delight friends with their beautifully decorated Christmas trees.

In 1880 no one could have predicted the success of glass blown ornaments which were just beginning to be imported by a few American stores. F.W. Woolworth, the great merchant who invented the five-and-ten cent store, failed to realize that glass ornaments would soon make him a substantial part of his fortune. At that time Woolworth had only one store located at Lancaster, Pennsylvania. From his log Woolworth stated:

> In the fall of 1880 I went to an importing firm on Strawberry Street, Philadelphia to buy some toys and about the first

thing they did was drag a lot of colored glass ornaments the thing of which I had never seen. "What are those things?" I asked ---"You can't sell me any foolish thing like that," I said. "I don't believe they would sell and most of them would be smashed anyway before there was a chance to sell them." They explained the profit was big enough to offset the breakage, but I was incredulous. It was hard to understand what the people would want of those colored glass things. We argued back and forth a long time and finally the house made me the proposition that it would guarantee the sale, at retail, of twenty five dollars worth of Christmas tree ornaments. "All right," I agreed. " You can send them to me wholly at your own risk."

The goods arrived a few days before Christmas and, with a great deal of indifference, I put them on my counters. In two days they were gone, and I woke up. But it was too late to order any more, and I had to turn away a big demand. The next Christmas season I was on hand early with what I considered a large order, but it was not large enough. They proved to be the best sellers in my store for the holiday.

In 1890, ten years after his first small ornament order and sale, he traveled to Lauscha, Germany. This was the village that made the first glass-blown ornaments. That year he bought more than two hundred thousand ornaments.

Customers in those days bought ornaments as individual pieces not in boxes of a dozen as they would do years later. Rope garlands of tinsel started to be sold to accompany the beautiful glass ornaments.

Another glittering product that is still being used today are "icicles" first made and sold in Nuremberg, Germany in 1878. These were the strips of silver foil designed to hang from decorated boughs like real "icicles". Users were divided into two groups, "hangers" and "throwers". One problem developed with these icicles. When cigarette smoke touched them they would turn black. Americans then developed a method to combat the blackening by producing lead-foil icicles. In 1960 the U.S. Government became concerned about lead poisoning of children who might swallow tinsel. The government forced the companies to abandon lead foil. Aluminum was not successful, so the manufacturers turned to light-weight silver-colored mylar.

We can thank Germany also for "angel hair" which was developed about 1880. It could be used as rope garland or spread out to cover the entire tree for a cobweb affect.

The use of romantic pictures known as "Scraps" began to be used on the Christmas tree. Pictures might be the "Nativity", cherubs, and beautiful angels with long, golden hair, Christmas trees, and old-fashioned Santa Claus figures. Many scraps had an addition of tinsel or angel hair.

Other Christmas ornaments started to be made of cotton wool or cotton batting and folded or glued over wire on a cardboard frame. Then placed over this would be printed faces of Santa, or angels, or little girls with curly hair. The advantage of these were that they were unbreakable objects that the children were allowed to touch.

Between 1870 and 1910 many tree ornaments made in Germany were made from bright and shiny wire and then made into stars, butterflies, and rosettes.

The ornament at the top of the tree was always important. Glass-blown "treetops" or "points" up to fourteen inches long became available. This most difficult ornament was free-blown from a single piece of glass tubing.

Soon after the outbreak of World War I the allies put an embargo on German products. The shelves became bare of German ornaments. American fast made ornaments came into existence but they were crude and poorly done. In the early 1920's Germany again regained the market.

In 1930 in New York City Max Eckart, an importer of German Christmas ornaments could see problems brewing in Germany. He convinced

Corning Glass Company to take up the mass production of machine-made Christmas balls.

In 1926 Eckart built a large factory called "Brothers Eckardt" which specialized in wooden toys and glass Christmas tree ornaments. After World War II his business became America's largest importer and manufacturer of Christmas tree ornaments.

Eckardt really started to sense problems developing in Germany. He went to Corning Glass in New York to talk to them about his idea of starting an American based glass ornament business. Corning had a "ribbon" glass blowing machine developed for the manufacturing of electric light bulbs. Eckardt reasoned that the machine ought to be able to blow Christmas tree ornaments.

Woolworth and Eckardt convinced Corning to adapt its bulb machine to ornament making. In 1939 the first 235,000 ornaments were shipped to Woolworth's. The following year big cartons were sent to Eckardt.

With the World War II war shortages it was impossible to get lacquer or silver for decorating. Soon metal for caps and hangers was not available.

Following the war Eckardt's trade name was "Shiny Brite" and it became the biggest ornament company in the world.

In the late 1960's Corning returned to decorating ornaments in its own plants while continuing to supply "blanks" to Shiny Brite and other finishers. Corning still produces most of the glass ornaments made in America.

There are many, many choices for trimming the tree. There are as many as your imagination will allow. They can be homemade decorations, ornaments purchased in a store, or a combination of both.

HOW "MERRY CHRISTMAS" IS WRITTEN AROUND THE WORLD

Following are a few examples of how Merry Christmas is written around the world:

Belgium (Flemish)	Vrolijke Kerstmis
China	Kung Hsi Hsin Nien or Bing Chu Shen Tan
Czechoslovakia	Vesele Vanoce
Denmark	Glaedelig Jul
Finland	Hauskaa Joulua
France	Joyeux Noel
Germany	Frohliche Weinachten
Holland	Zalig Kerstfeest
Italy	Bono Natale
Mexico	Feliz Navidad
Sweden	Glad Jul

GIFT-GIVERS OF CHRISTMAS IN TRADITION

There have been many names given to "gift-givers" of Christmas. Following are a few examples:

Austria	Saint Nicholas or Christkindl
Belgium	Saint Nicholas
Brazil	Papa Noël
England	Father Christmas
France	Père Noël or le Petit Jesus
Holland	Saint Nicholas
Italy	Befana
Mexico	Three Kings
Puerto Rico	Santa Claus and Wise Men
Spain	Wise Men
Switzerland	Christkind, Saint Nicholas or Father Christmas and Lucy
U.S.A.	Santa Claus

GIFT-GIVING DAYS

Most families in the United States open gifts on Christmas Eve or Christmas Day. Other countries, however, exchange gifts on different days. Following are some examples:

Austria	Saint Nicholas Day and Christmas
England	Christmas or December 26th (Boxing Day)
France	Christmas for children's gifts, New Year's for adults
Holland	Saint Nicholas Day
Italy	Epiphany, January 6
Mexico	Epiphany
Spain	Epiphany
Sweden	Saint Lucia's Day, December 13

NICHOLAS

According to biographies of Nicholas, written long after his death, he was born in Patara in Asia Minor about 280 A.D. His parents were married many years when finally they were blessed with a child. He was christened in the Roman Catholic Church as Nicholas which means "victorious, hero of the people" in Greek. He enjoyed school and faithfully attended religious services. At ages of twelve to thirteen (some sources say nine) his happy life was shattered when a plague hit Patara and both his parents died leaving him an orphan.

Because of his religious convictions he started giving away to charity his inheritance, which was quite extensive for the day. He also continued devoting himself to religious studies. At age nineteen he was ordained a priest and soon became Bishop of Myra, a city near Patara. Because of his young age he was often called the "Boy Bishop".

Nicholas soon became known as a very kind man with great wisdom. The church really flourished until 303 when emperor Diocletian commanded all citizens of the Roman Empire, which included Asia Minor, to worship him as a god. The emperor warned that they would be imprisoned and tortured unless they gave in. Thousands of Christians including Nicholas were imprisoned. Nicholas was confined to a small cell for five years. When he was released he returned to his post as

Bishop of Myra and remained there until the end of his life. He died December 6, 343 and soon after became known as Saint Nicholas by the people of the area.

Around the year 800 A.D. Nicholas was officially recognized as a saint by the Eastern Catholic Church. In the eyes of the Catholic Church, a saint is someone who has lived such a holy life that after dying and going to heaven, he or she is still able to help people on earth.

Nicholas became the patron saint to sailors, merchants, marriageable maidens, and children. Sailors on ships from all over the world spread the word of the wonderful deeds of Nicholas. Soon the Bishop of Myra began to change into the gift-giver we know today.

In many Catholic countries Saint Nicholas kept the gift-giver role on December sixth but in Protestant countries the gift-giving moved to Christmas or even Epiphany which is January sixth.

It's interesting to know that many churches were named in honor of Nicholas, in fact, over 400 churches in England were named for him.

Saint Nicholas
Born A.D. 280 - Died A.D. 343

THE CREATION OF SANTA CLAUS

Not everyone in America knew about Santa Claus at the beginning of the 1800's. Christmas wasn't even celebrated in many parts of the new nation. It depended from what country in Europe the colonists had come and what religious traditions they had brought with them.

In America, Santa Claus was in a way imported from Europe in the names of Father Christmas, Sinter Klaas, Papa Nöel, and Kris Kringle.

Four men - John Pintard, Washington Irving, Clement Clark Moore, and Thomas Nast - were largely responsible for Santa's popularity.

John Pintard was a man who loved holidays. An interesting point - it is due to his efforts that we celebrate Washington's birthday and the Fourth of July. He also got the New Yorkers of all nationalities interested in the early Dutch "Sinter Claes" (Sint meaning "Saint" Claes, a shortened form of "Nicholas".)

Next came Washington Irving who wrote *History of New York from the Beginning of the New World to the End of the Dutch Dynasty.* Irving constantly made mention of Saint Nicholas in his book which was a mixture of fact and fiction. Irving's Nicholas was no Bishop but a sturdy Dutch man wearing a hat and smoking a pipe. Irving introduced Nicholas to many Americans who had never heard of him before.

Missing from Irving's account was Black Peter so this figure never became a part of Nicholas in the New World.

Among those who read, enjoyed, and remembered Irving's portrayal of Saint Nicholas was Clement Clark Moore, author of the beloved Christmas poem, *A Visit From St. Nicholas*. He would center it on a portrayal of Saint Nicholas, inspired by the fat, jolly old Dutch handyman who used to work on the Moore family's estate. The idea that he rode in a sleigh pulled by reindeer came from an anonymous poem that was published in a collection, *The Children's Friend*, in 1821, a year before Moore wrote his. The poem began:

> Old Santeclaus with much delight
> His reindeer drives this frosty night
> O'er chimney-tops and tracks of snow
> To bring his yearly gifts to you.

Moore may have known the poem from reading to his children; however instead of a single reindeer who pulled the sleigh, Moore gave the famous team "eight tiny reindeer."

Moore also probably had heard some of the old Dutch stories and poems about Saint Nicholas and Black Peter. In these stories Black Peter came down the chimney and brought the presents. Moore also may have read about the Swedish Christmas elf called Jul since he described Nicholas as looking like an elf. Also bits of imagery - the pipe, the smoke, the "laying a finger aside of his nose" - are taken directly from Irving's *History*. It is likely that Irving's writings may have inspired Moore to make Nicholas "chubby and plump," the very opposite of the lean bishop shown in paintings. Also it probably was Germany's Pelznickle that caused him to be dressed all in fur from his head to his toe." Moore took all these elements and made an entirely new creation. With the mounting interest in Christmas and Santa Claus, his physical appearance was not entirely clear to adults and children alike.

Thomas Nast, a German born illustrator and cartoonist, responded by doing a series of Christmas drawings that appeared in Harper's Weekly magazine in 1863 and continued until 1886, twenty-three years of helping Americans with a "picture" of Santa Claus.

Nast's Santa was clearly based on Moore's since he was "chubby and plump", "dressed all in fur from his head to his foot", " beard was as white as the snow", he smoked a pipe and carried his "bundle of toys" which were "flung on his back."

Nast also added details of his own, like the North Pole workshop where the toys were made. Also Nast started the idea that Santa had a great book in which all children's names were recorded, along with notes about their behavior and also that Santa answered stacks of letters that children wrote to him.

Thomas Nast's first published drawing of Santa Claus, from Christmas Poems, 1863-64 (Culver Pictures).

Peeking to See Santa
Thomas Nast - December, 1870

Santa Claus reading letters from children. Drawing by Thomas Nast. (Notice the letters are coming from the children's parents.)

"Merry Old Santa Claus"
By Thomas Nast, January 1, 1881

"At the Shrine of Santa Claus - We Are All Good Children."
(Note - Saint Nicholas as an elf and at the North Pole)

Most artists and illustrators who followed Nast stayed within the traditions he had established. But in 1889 Mrs. Santa Claus made her appearance in a book entitled, *Goody Santa Claus on a Sleigh Ride* by Katherine Lee Bates, who later wrote "America the Beautiful."

Santa's image was updated in 1931 when Haddon Sundblom began a series of colored paintings commissioned by the Coca Cola Company. He followed Moore's description except his Santa was large, grandfatherly, and well over six foot. The elf look started to disappear.

In 1939 another dimension was added to Santa Claus and his Christmas trip to all the homes of boys and girls. Robert May, a copyrighter for Montgomery Ward and Company created Rudolph the Red-Nosed Reindeer. When the company no longer was interested in Rudolph, they gave the copyright to May who sent the story to Johny Marks, a songwriter. Marks wrote the song; Gene Autry sang it, and it climbed to the top of the Hit Parade. Rudolph's fame increased when in 1964 an animated film of his adventures was televised.

Rudolph, the Red-Nosed Reindeer,
Had a Very Shiny Nose.

Santa was introduced throughout Europe and Asia during the wars when American GIs made Santa known and loved. Except in the Netherlands, where loyalty to Saint Nicholas is strong, Santa is making inroads replacing many of his ancestors, both Christian and pagan.

In the early 1900's, people began to focus on the needs of children. Soon the notion arose that every child had the right to a joyful Christmas and Santa seemed the means to get this accomplished. Men dressed as Santa appeared everywhere - Santas for the Salvation army and department stores and malls and Santas for those fun private parties.

Soon special training schools were set up to teach people how to play Santa Claus. In 1956 a national retail organization issued a list of guidelines for department store Santa Clauses and their proper behavior.

Thousands and thousands of individuals each year devote themselves to playing Santa Claus so children can have some joy during the Christmas season.

Whether Santa gets fatter or thinner, or travels by space ship instead of reindeers, no doubt he will remain the world's most beloved symbol of cheer and generosity.

THAT WONDERFUL CLEMENT CLARK MOORE

Clement Clark Moore was a man of many talents. Besides writing light verse, he was an accomplished musician and professor of Greek and Hebrew literature at the General Theological Seminary in New York City. He was a learned man, serious, perhaps even solemn. He was also the father of six children.

According to his granddaughter, Moore got the idea for *A Visit from Saint Nicholas* while riding home one December evening in 1822 in a sleigh filled with presents for his six children all of whom were under seven years of age. That Christmas Eve he read it aloud to his family. The children loved it and he was quite satisfied with it.

As stated elsewhere in the book Moore borrowed ideas from other authors but also added some very creative additions to the poem. It was an entirely new creation!

After reading the poem to his family and some of their guests, a young women named Harriet Butler asked for a copy. Much to Moore's shock his friend Harriet sent it to the *Troy Sentinal* and it was published December 23, 1823 without identifying the author and accompanied by a note:

"We know not to whom we are indebted for this description of that unwearied patron of children - that homely and delightful personage of parental kindness - Santa Claus... but from whomsoever it may have come, we give thanks for it."

One of the reasons Moore did not want his poem published was because he was a Professor of Divinity and in those days people in his position were not to have any secular thoughts.

In the next few years the poem was reprinted in many other papers and the readers were constantly wanting to know who the author was. In 1929 the editor of the *Troy Sentinal* announced that the author was "a gentleman and scholar of the city of New York" but they didn't name Moore.

It was not until 1837 that Moore finally brought himself to acknowledge publicly that he was the author. In 1844 he also included it in an anthology of his poems. He probably never realized the importance of his contributions to Christmas.

Old Chelsea mansion house

Clement Clarke Moore's homestead, Chelsea House, in midtown Manhattan, is where he wrote the famous poem and first read it to his children on Christmas Eve, 1822. The drawing was made by Moore's daughter, Mary, some thirty-five years later.

CHRISTMAS GREENS AND FLOWERS

To the ancient Druids " the plants that do not die" were sacred, a symbol of life itself.

The ancient Romans decked their homes with evergreens at the Saturnalia celebration (December seventeenth to twenty-fourth) and at the Kalends of January, their New Year. Friends gave each other greenery for good fortune. (In the pagan celebration section of this book this is discussed in detail).

Long before there was a Christmas, primitive tribes in Europe hung evergreens above their doors during the winter season. Of course, we in the twentieth century use wreaths and garlands of pine, holly, mistletoe, and other greenery on our front doors, offices, stores, classrooms, and churches. It has become a part of our Christmas decoration tradition. Beautiful flowers have also joined in the beauty and meaning of the season.

THE POINSETTIA

The poinsettia comes in many colors such as red, pink, white, and speckled. The colored part of the plant is not the flower but is the bracts or leaves. The actual flowers of the poinsettia are the cluster of small yellow buds in the center of the leaves.

Most poinsettias come from California, particularly the poinsettias belts, where they are raised for use as Christmas gifts and decorations. The city of Ventura, California is even called Poinsettia

City. The town of Encinitas, California is known as the poinsettia capital of the world because of the super abundance of the flower there. Each Christmas they sponsor "Poinsettia Tours" to view the beautiful, large plants.

In Central America and Mexico this plant is known as the "Flame Leaf" or "Flower of the Holy Night". In Mexico it is prized because of its appearance in a popular legend. In Mexico people take flowers on Christmas Eve and place them in Christ's manger. One year a poor boy was brokenhearted because he had no flowers to take to church. An angel appeared to him and told him to pick some weeds from the side of the road. The boy did as instructed and brought the weeds to the church. When he placed them in the manger, they changed into scarlet flowers.

From 1825-1829 Dr. Joel Roberts Poinsett was the American ambassador to Mexico. Being a botanist he became very interested in the poinsettia and brought it back to his home in South Carolina. It became very popular and was named "Poinsettia" in honor of Dr. Joel Robert Poinsett.

It was discovered by Dr. Poinsett that this plant must, to set buds and produce flowers, have fourteen hours of continuous darkness for at least seventy-five to eighty days.

"Flower of the Holy Night"

POINSETTIAS
J. Harold Gwynne

We hail you, lovely Christmas flower,
With scarlet petals bright;
How graciously you bear your name:
"The Flower of Holy Night!"

Your beauty takes the breath away!
In fields of brilliant blooms;
In gaily planted garden plots;
In quiet living rooms.

But most of all in every church,
    With chancel all aglow,
You thrill the hearts of worshippers,
    And wondrous beauty show.

You symbolize for all of us
    The hopes of Christmas Day:
You decorate our gifts of love,
    And brighten all our way.

Repeat the message that we need,
    Dear Flower of Holy Night;
Remind us of the Savior's love,
    And keep us in His light.

THE CHRISTMAS ROSE

    Until the twentieth century, the Christmas rose was grown in England - as the poinsettia is grown in America - as the Christmas flower. The flower is native to the mountains of Central Europe and it blooms in the coldest time of the year.
    The Christmas rose (Helleborus nigra) is not really a rose but is a member of the buttercup family. This pale white flower seems to rise miraculously from the cold winter earth, serving to remind us that life is full of miracles.
    Legends link this flower with the birth of Christ. As the legend goes a little shepherd girl

called Madelon of Bethlehem followed after the shepherds who had received the angel's message and were going to see the Christ Child. All the shepherds took along gifts for the baby, gifts such as fruits, honey, and a white dove. The little girl was so sad because she had no gift to take. Suddenly an angel appeared. She spread beautiful white roses for the shepherd girl. The little girl eagerly gathered them in her arms and laid them at the manger as a gift to the little Lord Jesus.

MISTLETOE

The hanging of mistletoe at Christmas and New Year's was one of the many pagan customs carried over into the Christian era, in this case, without any special reason, but simply as a charming custom. Mistletoe was once held sacred by all European peoples, the small plant grows as a parasite, clinging to the highest branches of oaks and other trees.

Many early peoples believed the mistletoe to be a magical plant with great powers. About 2200 years ago, a group of people called the Celts lived in what are now the British Isles and France. Their priests, called the Druids, killed animals and people as gifts to the gods. They wanted the gods to protect them from evil spirits. The Druids really believed that the mistletoe which did grow on oak trees had wonderful, powerful, and special powers. They thought that during winter the oak tree god lived in the mistletoe after the oak leaves fell. When the winter solstice came, the priests dressed in white climbed an oak tree and cut down the mistletoe with a golden sickle. The mistletoe had to be caught in a white cloth, so it would not touch the ground where the evil spirits would hurt it. Part of the mistletoe was placed on an altar as a gift to the gods and the rest was given to the people of the villages to hang over their doors for good luck and as a symbol of welcome and friendship. There were also ceremonies in which kisses beneath the mistletoe symbolized the ending of old grievances. The Druids called the mistletoe "all healers" as they thought if childless women and animals ate it they would be able to have children. They believed it cured epilepsy and would also heal skin ulcers and protect people from being poisoned.

Long after Christianity replaced many older religions, faith in mistletoe lived on. It was forbidden in churches as pagan but became a part of Christmas in many homes.

Today mistletoe is a symbol of Christmas joy. It is a practice to kiss and embrace under the mistletoe, a custom coming from Scandinavia. Kissing under the mistletoe was thought to heal pain, end bitter arguments, and bring good luck. In some areas mistletoe had limited powers. At each kiss a berry had to be removed from the hanging branch, and when the berries were gone the game was finished and more mistletoe had to be hung.

The English preserved the ancient tradition after others left it fade. Mistletoe was given the care and decoration we now lavish on our Christmas trees. A "kissing bunch" or "kissing ball" is constructed of two hoops, one thrust through the other. Each is garlanded with sprigs of green, decorated with colored ribbons, paper roses, apples, or oranges. Inside are placed three tiny figures to represent the crib scene. Finally mistletoe is tied to the bottom of the ball which is then hung in a doorway or prominent place.

Whether it works or not is not important. If it brings joy and fun and carries on an ancient custom, then it has its place in our Christmas and New Year.

Druids Catching the Mistletoe

HOLLY

The leaders of the early church wanted to get rid of the pagan custom of bringing evergreen indoors. But people, even after becoming Christians, did not want to stop using holly as a decoration. Finally the church decided to make evergreens, which includes holly, a part of the story of Christ's life. A legend began that the crown of thorns Christ wore before his death was made of holly leaves. When the crown pierced Christ's forehead, his blood flowed over the holly berries, changing them from white to red.

Because the plant had also come to stand for peace and joy, people often settled quarrels under and around holly. Plants near the home were to frighten off evil spirits and witches and protect a building from thunder and lightning. A sprig of holly on the bedpost was thought to bring happy dreams.

A Sprig of Holly

IVY

As was mentioned holly was finally accepted by the church when they gave it religious significance. Ivy, on the other hand, took much longer to be accepted because it was the symbol of an ancient Roman god named Bacchus who was the god of wine. Since the church didn't approve of drunkenness, the symbol was not brought into the early church. As time passed ivy became a symbol for everlasting and eternal life and thus became accepted and used as a Christmas decoration. The holly and the ivy are mentioned together many times because they were symbols for the male and female halves of human nature.

The early English Christmas carol *The Holly and the Ivy* shows that they were accepted by the church and had become part of the Christmas story by the sixteenth century:

Ivy, Symbol of Eternal Life

The Holly and the Ivy

The holly and the ivy,
When they are both full grown,
Of all the trees that are in the wood,
The holly bears the crown:

> Chorus
> The rising of the sun
> And the running of the deer,
> The playing of the merry organ,
> Sweet singing in the choir.

The holly bears a blossom,
As white as lily flower,
And Mary bore sweet Jesus Christ
To do poor sinners good.
> Chorus

The holly bears a prickle,
As sharp as any thorn,
And Mary bore sweet Jesus Christ
On Christmas Day in the morn.
> Chorus

The holly bears a bark,
As bitter as any gall,
And Mary bore sweet Jesus Christ
For to redeem us all.
> Chorus

LAUREL

In ancient Rome, the first Christians decorated their homes during the winter solstice with laurel, or bay, as well as holly. Among the pagans, laurel was sacred to Apollo, the sun god. Laurel continued to be used as a symbol by the early Christians.

ROSEMARY

There are several things that are very special about rosemary. It has a sweet, pleasant aroma, it has a beautiful gray-green color, and it can be used as a flavoring for foods.

According to tradition, rosemary, received its fragrance when Mary hung Jesus's baby blankets over it and also laid other garments of His on its branches. The legend goes on to say the herb received its color from Mary's cloak which she also placed on the branches.

In the Middle Ages, housewives spread it on the floors so their houses would have a nice aroma. By the nineteenth century, the herb was used in England to flavor the boar's head that was cooked for the Christmas feast. Now, it is used primarily as a food seasoning.

Yes, the use of plants and greenery as winter decorations began long before Christ was born. They have an interesting history and even now bring beauty during the Christmas season.

THE CHRISTMAS CALENDAR

Many people believe Christmas is a one-day holiday or festival while others believe it lasts for twelve days. Also an important time for Christians is Advent which starts on the fourth Sunday before Christmas and ends on Christmas Day.

December sixth is Saint Nicholas Day honored because it was the day of his death in 343 A.D. (Earlier in the book is a section on Saint Nicholas.)

Saint Lucia's Day is December thirteenth, the beginning of the Christmas season in Sweden, that lasts a whole month. Lucia was a young girl who was put to death in Sicily in 304 A.D. for professing Christianity.

Spanish-speaking Americans also emphasize the nine days before Christmas called the "posadas" days. During these nine days, people act out Mary and Joseph's search for the inn in Bethlehem. Then on Christmas Day a doll is added to the manger scene to stand for Christ's birth.

Boxing Day is held December twenty-sixth and is a legal holiday in England. On this day boxes of food and clothing are gathered and given to those less fortunate. This is also the Feast of Saint Stephen.

Christmas is celebrated on January seventh by many Greek and Russian Orthodox churches. On the Gregorian calendar, which they follow, January seventh is the same as December twenty-fifth.

The twelve days of Christmas begin on Christmas Eve and last until Epiphany on January sixth. Epiphany was an early Roman festival that honored the Magi's visit to Bethlehem. Today Epiphany mainly marks the end of the Christmas season. It is the time to take down decorations in the church and also in the home.

A few churches keep their decorations up until February second, the Feast of Candlemas. On this day candles are blessed for the coming year.

CHRISTMAS CALENDAR

The fourth Sunday before Christmas
    First day of Advent
December 6
    Saint Nicholas's Day
December 13
    Saint Lucia's Day
December 16-25
    Posadas days
December 24
    Christmas Eve
December 25
    Christmas Day
December 26
    Feast of Saint Stephen and Boxing Day
January 5
    Epiphany Eve
January 6
    Epiphany
January 7
    Greek and Russian Orthodox Christmas
February 2
    Candlemas

THE STORY OF THE TWELVE DAYS OF CHRISTMAS

The Christmas carol, *The Twelve Days of Christmas,* never makes sense until the readers discover the explanation of why it was written. I thought it strange to have nine ladies dancing and ten lords a leaping along with a partridge who sat up in a pear tree. But this song is more than a tune with pretty phrases and strange gifts. It is a song with deep levels of meaning and shows how the Christian church has had to teach and spread the Gospel in times of persecution.

From 1558 until 1829 Roman Catholics in England were not allowed to practice their faith openly. During this time, this song was written as a catechism song for young believers. It has two levels of meaning: the surface meaning with these strange gifts plus a hidden meaning known only to members of their church. The hidden meaning of the song's gifts were intended to help the children remember lessons of their faith. Each element in the carol has a code word for a religious reality.

Instead of referring to an earthly suitor, the "true love" mentioned in the song refers to God himself. The "me" who receives the presents is symbolic of every baptized believer. The partridge in the pear tree is Jesus Christ. In the song Christ is symbolically presented as a mother partridge which feigns injury to decoy predators from her helpless nestlings. The meanings of the other symbols are:

- Two Turtle Doves - The Old and New Testaments
- Three French Hens - Faith, Hope, and Love
- Four Calling Birds - The four Gospels (Matthew, Mark, Luke, and John)
- Five Golden Rings - The first five books of the Old Testament which give the history of man's fall from grace
- Six Geese-a-Laying - the six days of creation
- Seven Swans-a-Swimming - Seven gifts of the Holy Spirit
- Eight Maids-a-Milking - The Eight Beatitudes
- Nine Ladies Dancing - Nine fruits of the Holy Spirit
- Ten Lords-a-Leaping - The Ten Commandments
- Eleven Pipers Piping - The eleven faithful disciples
- Twelve Drummers Drumming - The twelve points of belief in the Apostle's Creed

As the author of this book it is my hope the next time you hear or sing this song you will have a new found respect and understanding of this wonderful and meaningful Christmas tradition.

THE TWELVE DAYS OF CHRISTMAS

On the first day of Christmas my true love sent to me
A partridge in a pear tree.

On the second day of Christmas my true love sent to me, Two turtle doves and a partridge in a pear tree.

On the third day of Christmas my true love sent to me, Three french hens, two turtle doves, and a partridge in a pear tree.

On the fourth day of Christmas my true love sent to me, Four calling birds ....

On the fifth day of Christmas my true love sent to me Five gold rings ....

On the sixth day of Christmas my true love sent to me Six geese a-laying ....

On the seventh day of Christmas my true love sent to me, Seven swans a-swimming ....

On the eighth day of Christmas my true love sent to me, Eight maids a-milking ....

On the ninth day of Christmas my true love sent to me, Nine drummers drumming ....

On the tenth day of Christmas my true love sent to me, Ten pipers piping ....

On the eleventh day of Christmas my true love sent to me, Eleven ladies dancing ....

On the twelfth day of Christmas my true love sent to
me, Twelve lords a-leaping,
    Eleven ladies dancing,
    Ten pipers piping,
    Nine drummers drumming,
    Eight maids a-milking,
    Seven swans a-swimming,
    Six geese a-laying,
    Five gold rings,
    Four calling birds,
    Three French hens,
    Two turtle doves,
    And a partridge in a pear tree.
                      Traditional English Carol

THE STORY OF SILENT NIGHT

The Napoleonic Wars were over, peace reigned in Austria with a wonderful silence and beauty on a winter night. This was the setting for the writing of *Silent Night*. It was written on Christmas Eve, 1818, in the village of Obendorf, near Salzburg, Austria in the Alps.

There are different stories as to what occurred just prior to the writing of this famous Christmas carol. One said that Joseph Mohr a young priest was alone on Christmas Eve. A loud pounding on the door brought a woman asking him to come to a home high in the Alps. He went to the small cabin and saw a "repetition of the Nativity Scene" that had happened many years ago in Bethlehem. He blessed the cabin and the family and returned to his rectory. On the way home his heart was filled with song and he felt a beautiful rhythm. He stayed up late writing the words. In the morning he rushed to the church organist, Fanz Gruber, asking him to set to music the poem he had just written. To his dismay Franz told Joseph that the organ could not be played. One source says that because the church was so near the Salzach River, rust caused serious problems to the organ. Most sources say that mice had nibbled at the bellows causing a malfunction. Regardless the organ could not be used that Christmas. Both Franz and Mohr decided it would be a fine idea to set the poem to music that could be sung by the choir and accompanied on a guitar. That they did. On

December 25, 1818 the village people met at the church for mass and heard *Silent Night* for the first time. Mohr with his tenor voice and Gruber with his bass voice and guitar sang with the choir. Neither ever knew, that they had achieved immortality with their Christmas carol. This hymn has been translated into over 100 different languages and dialects.

In 1818 the hymn was called *Holy Night! Peaceful Night!* and of course was written in the German language. In 1863 John F. Young translated it, dropped one verse, and entitled it *Silent Night! Holy Night!*

How sad it is that Father Mohr died in poverty in Salzburg on December 4, 1848. Ironically his skull rests beneath the Nativity Scene in Oberdorf's Silent Night Chapel which is located on the site of Saint Nicholas Church, the church where *Silent Night* was first heard.

HOLY NIGHT! PEACEFUL NIGHT!

Holy Night, peaceful night,
All is dark, save the light
Yonder where they sweet vigil keep
 O'er the Babe, who in silent sleep,
Rests in heavenly peace, Rests in heavenly peace.

Silent night, holiest night,
Darkness flies, all is light,
Shepherds hear the angels sing:

"Alleluia! hail the King,
Christ the Savior is here, Jesus the Savior is here."

Silent night, holiest night,
Guiding Star, lend thy light!
See the eastern wise men bring,
Gifts and homage to our King,
Christ the Savior is here, Jesus the Savior is here.

Silent night, holiest night,
Wondrous Star, lend thy light!
With an angel let us sing,
Alleluia to our King,
Christ the Saviour is here, Jesus the Saviour is here.
Amen

SILENT NIGHT! HOLY NIGHT!

Silent night! holy night!
All is calm, all is bright
'Round yon virgin mother and Child,
Holy Infant so tender and mild,
Sleep in heavenly peace, Sleep in heavenly peace.

Silent night! holy night!
Shepherds quake at the sight,
Glories stream from heaven afar,
Heav'nly hosts sing Alleluia;
Christ the Savior is born, Christ the Savior is born.

Silent night! holy night!
Son of God, love's pure light,
Radiant beams from Thy holy face,
With the dawn of redeeming grace,
Jesus, Lord, at Thy birth, Jesus, Lord, at Thy birth.
Amen

STILLE NACHT

Stille Nacht, helilge Nacht!
Alles schlaeft cinsam wacht
Nur das traute hochheilige Paar.
Holder Knabe im lockigem Haar,
Schlaf in himmlischer Ruh!

Stille Nacht, heilige Nacht,
Hirten erst kund gemacht!
Durch der Engel Hallelujah
Toent es laut von fern und nah:
Christ der Retter ist da!

Stille Nacht, hoilige Nacht,
Gottes Sohn, O wie lacht
Lieb aus deinem goettlichen Mund
Da uns schlaegt die rettende Stund,
Christ in deiner Geburt!

THE STORY OF THE CANDY CANE

The traditional candy stick was born over 350 years ago when mothers used white sugar sticks as pacifiers for their babies. Around 1670, the choirmaster of Cologne Cathedral in Cologne, Germany bent the sticks into canes to represent a shepherd's staff. He then used these white candy canes to keep the attention of small children during the long Nativity service.

The use of candy canes during the Christmas season spread throughout Europe. In Northern Europe, sugar canes decorated with sugar roses were used to brighten the home at Christmas time.

In the mid 1800's the candy cane arrived in the United States where a German-Swedish immigrant in Wooster, Ohio, decorated his Christmas tree with paper ornaments and white sugar canes.

The red stripe was added to the candy cane at the turn of the century when peppermint was added and became a traditional flavor for candy.

Some sources say that a candy maker in Indiana developed the candy cane as a witness of Christ's love. To do something special for Jesus's birthday, he incorporated several symbols for the birth, ministry, and death of Jesus Christ.

He began with a stick of pure white, hard candy. White to symbolize the virgin birth and the sinless nature of Jesus, and hard to symbolize the solid rock, the foundation of the church, and the firmness of the promises of God.

The candy maker made the candy in the form of a "J" to represent the precious name of Jesus, who came to earth as a Savior. It could also represent the staff of the "good shepherd" with which he reaches down into the world to lift out the fallen lambs who, like all sheep, have gone astray.

Thinking that the candy cane was somewhat plain, the candy maker stained it with red stripes. He wanted to emphasize the scripture that said, by Jesus stripes we are healed and Jesus was beaten and stripes were put upon His back when he was crucified in payment for our sins. So the candy cane was made with red and white stripes to represent the blood of Jesus which washes away our sins and makes us white as snow. One bold red stripe represents our belief in one God who is Father of us all and for the blood shed by Christ on the cross so that we could have the promise of eternal life. The three fine small red stripes are to show the stripes of the scourging Jesus received and also the Trinity; one God who has revealed Himself to us in three ways: The Father, the Son, and the Holy Spirit.

Unfortunately the candy has become known as a *cane*, a meaningless decoration at Christmas time. The meaning is still there for those who "have eyes to see and ears to hear."

There are lots of candy canes in the stores today made with different colors but they are not true candy canes unless they are red and white and have *one* bold stripe and *three* fine stripes.

True candy canes are Christian candy because they tell the story of Jesus.

Show your love this Christmas season by only buying and giving *Christian candy*, a true candy cane, to your friends and loved ones.

While we may never know the full history of the candy cane, we can share in the truth behind its symbolism, the truth of Christ's birth and redemption, and the gift of His love.

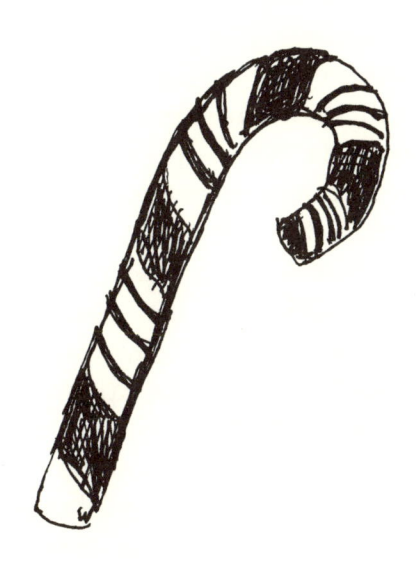

Christian Candy Cane

THE HISTORY OF THE CHRISTMAS CARDS

Christmas cards whether secular or sacred are a wonderful way to keep in touch with one another. Many times friends will include a letter or some snapshots. The predecessor of the Christmas cards are "Christmas Pieces", which was started in England by British school boys. These were elaborate colored sheets of paper with Bible scenes around the outside. In the middle the children wrote, in their finest penmanship, a Christmas note to their parents along with their signature. Supposedly this was to put parents in a wonderful, giving mood so they would be generous with their Christmas presents and also to show their parents how diligent their studies in school had been. Sometimes adults would also write Christmas verses to their friends.

Two things made the advent of the Christmas card so popular. One was the "penny post" by the British postal system in 1840. This made sending the cards possible and relatively inexpensive. The other was the great increase in printing in the nineteenth century because of the invention of the printing press.

Sir Henry Cole an Englishman has been credited with the first Christmas card. In 1843 he hired an artist named J.C. Horsley to draw a picture of a family happily sipping wine. Next to the picture he wrote, "A Merry Christmas and a Happy New Year." Sir Henry Cole printed and sold a thousand copies. These were printed, colored by hand, and sold for a shilling apiece. Soon a number of companies were printing Christmas cards. On them were cupids, robins, flowers, holly, mistletoe, Father Christmas, and winter snow scenes.

The first Christmas card, 1843,
designed by J.C. Horsley

Soon the Christmas card found its way to the United States. Louis Prang, a German born printer, working in his shop in Roxbury, Massachusetts, printed the first American cards in 1875. He really popularized the card by having a nationwide contest for the best designs and awarding cash prizes. His early designs were quite simple but they became fancier as time passed.

    Sending Christmas cards has become an American custom with billions sent each year. A display may be put on a tree or on a wall or table, or wherever the family would so desire. An exchange of cards often keeps alive a friendship or sometimes mends a broken friendship. Christmas is a season for reaching out to others and sharing a friendly hello.

THE HISTORY OF THE CHRISTMAS SEALS

The familiar Christmas seal originated in Denmark. A postal clerk Elinan Holboell noticed a tremendous volume of Christmas mail. While stamping letters and Christmas cards in 1903 at Copenhagen, an idea occurred to him. He was the kind of person who was saddened by the number of children suffering from tuberculosis. A question came into his thoughts. Why not add one cent to each letter and parcel and then give this money to build badly needed hospitals for those stricken with the dreaded disease? Why not have a special Christmas seal printed? Several prominent people expressed interest in the idea including King Christian. King Christian gave his approval and so the first Christmas seal came out during the Christmas season of 1904. Four million were sold that year yielding $18,000 for hospitals of tuberculosis patients.

Jacob Riis, a Danish immigrant to the United States, and a New York social worker, became a real enthusiast of the Danish seal program and introduced the idea to America. The seals did not become really successful in this country until 1910 when the National Tuberculosis Association (later known as the National Lung Association) took over the project. With the money from the seals, the prevention and treatment of patients has occurred and tuberculosis and other serious lung diseases have dropped tremendously as a cause of death.

For Christmas 1975, there were fifty-four different seals offered, each with a version of Santa Claus designed by a school child from every state and U.S. possession.

Examples of other organizations which now sell seals for their cause are the Easter Seals for Crippled Children and the America Bible Society.

Christmas Seals, 1975

CHRISTMAS STAMPS

The first postage stamp intended for Christmas was issued by Austria in 1937. It pictured a rose, a popular symbol in that country. After that Brazil, Hungary and other countries issued stamps. In 1959 the first set of stamps appeared from the Vatican. The United States issued its first Christmas stamp in 1962, a small green and red stamp showing a Christmas wreath and candles. The stamps are issued seasonly to give the mail some holiday spirit. The stamps, which benefit no organization but the United States Postal Service, feature different religious or secular Christmas scenes each year.

In 1971 a very popular stamp was produced. It was the reproduction of the *Adoration of the Shepherds* by an Italian painter Giorgione. Over one billion copies were printed.

Designs with religious signifigance have over the years proven to be the most popular.

THE MANY NAMES FOR THE MANGER SCENE

In the Middle Ages few people could read or write and the church services were all in Latin. Ways had to be found to teach the Bible stories. Figures showing the characters of Christmas like Mary, Joseph, Baby Jesus, kings, shepherds, angels, and animals of the stable were carved. Many of the early mangers in churches were very elaborate with gold, silver, and jewels. Saint Francis felt it was important for people to remember that Christ was born in a humble stable.

In 1207 the first recorded carved manger scene was done by Luigi in the town of Grecio in Italy. Luigi was a famous and excellent wood carver.

In 1223 Francis of Assisi asked a friend who lived in Grecio to take an oxen, donkey, manger and some straw to a nearby cave outside the town of Grecio. When this was done Francis, the Francisan Order of Friars, and the local people met by candle light in the cave on Christmas Eve. They acted out the story of Christ's birth. Francis told them to put hatred out of their hearts, and make Christmas a time of peace and goodwill. He then led the group in carol singing and asked the children to gather around the manger. The Christ Child, though life sized, was made of wax and was then put in the manger. It was even said that the people gave shouts of joy! Not long after his mass in Grecio on the hillside, Brother

Francis died. They have continued to re-create the scene as a symbol of hope, peace, and joy.

In a book called *The First Life of Saint Francis of Assisi* by Brother Thomas of Celano in 1229 A.D., he quoted Saint Francis when referring to the first manger scene in 1223:

> "For I would make a memorial of that Child who was born in Bethlehem, and in some sort behold with bodily eyes His infant hardships; how He lay in a manger on hay, with the ox and ass standing by."

As time went on people began setting up hand-carved manger scenes in their homes. From Italy it spread to Spain, France, Portugal and to all other parts of the Christian world. The Nativity scene became the center of Christmas celebrations in southern Europe just as the Christmas tree had in the north. The purpose of the manger scene was to help people understand the scripture so they might have deeper religious experiences.

Manger scenes have been given different names according to the country where they are made.

In France and United States we call it a crèche meaning cradle or manger. This word came from the Italian word Grecio, the town in which the famous manger scene was created by Saint Francis in the thirteenth century. In Italy it is called presepio or presepe which means manger. In Germany they use the word krippe again meaning manger and in Czechoslovakia they use jeslicky.

The custom of using the manger scene did not come to America until 1741 when the Moravians settled in Bethlehem, Pennsylvania. They displayed putzes which are large, fancy manger scenes brought from Germany. People from other nations also brought manger scenes to America. Now they are an important part of our Christmas season.

The Manger - Jesus's First Bed

SPIDERS AND CHRISTMAS

Several legends have grown during the ages concerning spiders and Christmas. One is a legend dealing with the golden spider webs and one dealing with the silver spider webs.

Once upon a time, long, long ago, a mother and her children busied themselves cleaning house for the most wonderful day of the year, Christmas. When they had finished, not a speck of dust remained. Even the friendly spiders had scampered from their cozy corners on the ceiling and fled to the attic.

At last it was Christmas Eve. The tree was decorated beautifully and the family had gone to sleep. The poor spiders, banished to the attic, were most unhappy that they could not see the special tree. The oldest and wisest spider looked around a bit and found a tiny crack just big enough for the spiders to squeeze through. One by one they crept silently into the room. The tree towered so high they could only see one ornament at a time. To get a better look, they scurried up the trunk and over every branch. When the spiders had finished their thorough inspection, the Christmas tree was shrouded in spider webs!!

Hearing the sounds of the family stirring, the tiny creatures deserted the dusty tree and retreated to their attic hideaway. Presently, from down below, came the sounds of delighted children. Their tree was shining with golden garland in the Christmas Day sun!

In many parts of the world, it has become a custom to have one golden spider on the Christmas tree.

Another legend concerning the spider explains why tinsel is used on the Christmas tree. Many years ago a good woman with a large family of children prepared the Christmas tree, trimming it profusely. During the night spiders visited the tree and crawled from branch to branch, leaving their beautiful webs behind them. To reward the woman for her goodness, the Christ Child blessed the tree and all the spider webs were transformed into shining silver.

Spider Legends

MUSIC OF CHRISTMAS

There was a renewed interest in the Christmas carols in England in the early nineteenth century. The Christmas-hating Puritans had suppressed the carols in the seventeenth century but glimpses of the carols survived especially in the west of England and in Wales. Two men Gilbert and Sandys saved such carols as *The First Noel, I Saw Three Ships*, and *God Rest Ye Merry, Gentlemen*. These men, through their writings, inspired a revival of interest in carols.

In 1751 John Francis Wade, an Englishman wrote *Adeste Fideles (O Come, All Ye Faithful.)* Isaac Watts, a Congregationalist minister in England who began writing hymns while in his teens, wrote *Joy to the World* in 1719. In 1739 Charles Wesley wrote *Hark! The Herald Angels Sing*. Wesley wrote more than 6,500 other hymns over the course of his lifetime.

William Dix, an insurance company executive and a fine poet in nineteenth century Scotland, wrote *What Child Is This?* and *As With Gladness Men of Old*. *As With Gladness Men of Old* was written because Dix was distressed by the legends that had grown up around the visit of the wise men. He set out to write a hymn in which the Magi would not be Kings or three in number. He simply wanted them to be "Men of Old."

A very familiar traditional carol recalls the carolers of Old England as they go from door to door, singing blessings on the house and asking for some good cheer in return.

There are numerous versions. In one version, "figgy pudding" is the reward sought, an unsweetened dish made with figs and often containing suet (fat), originally boiled in a bag, but now often steamed or boiled without a bag.

> We wish you a Merry Christmas,
> We wish you a Merry Christmas,
> We wish you a Merry Christmas
> And a Happy New Year!
>
> We want some figgy pudding,
> We want some figgy pudding,
> We want some figgy pudding
> And a cup of good cheer!
>
> We won't go until we get some,
> We won't go until we get some,
> We won't go until we get some,
> So bring it out here!
>
> We wish you a Merry Christmas,
> We wish you a Merry Christmas,
> We wish you a Merry Christmas,
> And a Happy New Year!

Between the surly third verse and the once again good-spirited fourth verse the carolers' wishes were granted and the cup of good cheer was brought out.

A number of well-known hymns came from the United States. *We Three Kings of Orient Are* was written by John Henry Hopkins, Jr. in 1859. Phillips Brooks while living in Pennsylvania wrote the words to *O Little Town of Bethlehem* for the children of his Sunday School.

Away in a Manger, frequently attributed to Martin Luther, seems to have originated among the German Lutherans in Pennsylvania.

And of course that best-loved song, *Silent Night* came from Austria and was written on Christmas Eve, 1818.

George Frederick Handel, an extremely gifted German composer and musician, began work on his famous oratorio *The Messiah* in August 1741 and completed the entire work in twenty-three days.

Peter Ilich Tchaikovsky, a Russian musician, wrote a wonderful ballad called *The Nutcracker* that has delighted generations of both children and adults.

There is no limit to what may become a part of Christmas whether sacred or secular. *Jingle Bells* was written by James Pierpont in 1857. Never once does it mention Christmas, yet it has become one of the favorite holiday songs.

Another song, featured on Christmas cards, is a recent addition to Christmas. The song was written by Katherine Davis in the 1940's. It was a song in which the music came first and then the words and was entitled *The Little Drummer Boy*.

White Christmas written by Irving Berlin is another relatively new Christmas song. It was first sung by Bing Crosby and was incorporated in a film called *Holiday Inn*. The film became an immediate hit.

If the music portrays the Wise Men, "The Babe", the candle, wreath, or mistletoe; or if it portrays the reindeer or poinsettia, all the symbolism varies but the message remains the same - joy, peace, love, and generosity.

HOW MORAVIANS CELEBRATE CHRISTMAS

The Moravian Church traces its origin to the movement for church reform led by John Huss, a preacher in one of Prague's largest churches. He felt the church of the day was no longer true to the gospel. This brought the condemnation of the church upon him and he was burned at the stake in 1415. Because much of the church, called the Unity of the Brethren, centered in Moravia the church later came to be known as the Moravian Church.

Because of a world-wide mission program, the Moravians came to America in 1735. In time they settled in Pennsylvania. On Christmas Eve, 1741, they chose the name Bethlehem for the central town of their settlement. In 1766 the Moravians founded Salem, North Carolina. The name Salem is derived from a Hebrew word for "peace." This historic area is now surrounded by the modern city of Winston-Salem.

The Moravians have intensive religious life, missionary zeal, handicraft industries, education, and a cultivation of music.

Christmas is an important time for the Moravians. Weeks before Christmas the housewives are busy in the kitchen preparing Kuemmelbrod, sugar cake, mince pies, and large quantities of Christmas cookies cut out in shapes dealing with Christmas symbols.

Everywhere there is music at Salem. Christmas bands play on the street corners, and in buildings are the sounds of violins, flutes, organs, harpsichords, and voices raised in song.

There are a number of customs of the early church that are still in practice today. One is the Easter sunrise service and the other is the love feast. The love feast was a part of the Christmas Eve observance at the founding of both Bethlehem, Pennsylvania and Salem, North Carolina. A love feast is a religious service in which Christian fellowship is emphasized. It is a song service during which the congregation has a simple meal of coffee and buns. This Christmas Eve love feast is impressive and moving. Following the sharing of food, there is a candle light service called an "Ode" in which all hearts are rededicated to Christ, the Light of the World. The beeswax candles are made by the women of the Moravian Church and the Mary Ann Fogle Service League.

The Moravian Christmas is distinguished by two forms of decoration - the star and the putz. (The star will be described later.) The word putz comes from the German word "putzer", to adorn or decorate. The putz really is a "Christmas yard" or "Christmas garden" with the Holy Family as the focal point. The miniatures are placed under the Christmas tree and really is a miniature landscape telling the story of Christ's birth. The putz may include dozens or even hundreds of figures, elaborate landscaping, waterfalls, houses, bridges, castles, and sawmills. The whole scene is lit up by miniature electric lights.

A person may visit a large putz at Central Moravian Church in Bethlehem, Pennsylvania. You may also visit Brothers House in Old Salem, North Carolina where their putz takes up two large rooms.

THE MORAVIAN STAR

A star, as part of the symbolism of Christmas, is as old as the season itself, since the star of Bethlehem figures so prominently in the nativity story. The use of the star by the Moravians is nothing unique. However, a particular type of star that originated in Germany over a hundred years ago has become associated with the way the Moravians celebrate Christmas.

The Moravian Star, a many pointed star, is also called the Advent Star or the Herrnhut Star. It is the custom to hang the star the first Sunday in Advent, preceding all other decorations, and keep it up until the Festival of Epiphany, January sixth, the traditional time of the coming of the Magi.

For a long time the Star was exclusively manufactured in Herrnhut, Germany thus the reason it is sometimes called the Herrnhut Star. The stars originally developed in boys' Moravian boarding schools as an evening handicraft, around 1850, in two villages - Niesky and Kleinwelka. Star making started as a exercise in geometry, gradually developing into an art.

Pieter Verbeeck, owner of a paper and music store in Herrnhut, was an alumni of the boys' school in Niesky and began to make the stars in his home for sale about the year 1900. He made a star that could be assembled. It had a metal frame and paper points on metal rims which were stuck onto a rigid frame. This star could be more easily packaged and transported than a star already put together. Later Pieter Verbeeck and his son Harry learned to make points which could be fastened together with paper fasteners, eliminating the rigid metal frame and making the star even easier to distribute.

Harry, founded the Herrnhut star factory, which soon developed into a thriving business sending his product to all parts of the world including the Moravian communities in Europe, the British Isles, America, and the scattered mission fields. He continued to supply Moravians in America with the stars until the start of World War I when his factory temporarily closed. After World War II, the star factory in Herrnhut, being in East Germany, was taken over and run by the communist government. It was returned to the Moravians in 1954. Today the factory is mechanized, but women in surrounding villages work there.

In America many stars are still obtained from Herrnhut, but many are hand-made in Salem, North Carolina and in Bethlehem, Pennsylvania which is called "The Christmas City." As stated earlier, during the period of World War II stars again could not be obtained from Herrnhut so local Moravian ministers began a project of taking supplies to shut-ins and disturbing the stars they made to local stores. Today local men and women make the stars for sale in various sizes. Some are obtained from Canada and some are still obtained from Herrnhut.

The first stars made in Kleinwelka and Niesky had alternating red and white points or alternating yellow and white points or were all red, but those shipped from Harry Verbeck's factory to America were all white. Stars can vary from as few as twenty points to as many as 110, although the traditional star has twenty-six points. The star is now made of plastic or of paper and can vary from ten inches in diameter to as large as twenty-two inches in diameter. When sent to customers it is usually sent with twenty-six points, wire hanging, fasteners, and instructions for assembling.

Early stars were lighted with small candles or grease lamps or a tiny cup of oil with a wick suspended inside. Now stars have an electric bulb inserted.

The Moravian Star

The Moravian Star is a reminder of the star that led the wise men to Bethlehem where they presented their gifts to the Christ Child (Matthew 2: v. 9). The star also symbolizes the Christ Child of whom the Old Testament prophesied, "A star shall come out of Jacob" (Numbers 24: v. 17). The Risen Christ, likewise, proclaimed himself as "The root and offspring of David, and the bright and morning star" (Revelation 22: v. 16).

The symbolic star is popular in both church and home. Its use has spread to hotels, stores, schools, hospitals, community displays, or wherever it has become customary to have Christmas decorations. Today Moravians and non-Moravians are displaying this beautiful star.

TRIVIA

1. Santa Claus has to visit more than two billion families in twenty-four hours. Reindeers have to travel at about 70,000 miles an hour. Santa can stay at each house for only one-half of one ten-thousandth of a second.

2. There really is a North Pole - at least three of them: Colorado, 80809; Alaska, 99705; New York, 12947.

3. For genuine Yule postmarks try:
   a. Christmas, Florida 32709
   b. Mistletoe, Kentucky 41351
   c. Rudolph, Ohio 43462
   d. Santa Claus, Indiana 47579
   e. Snowflake, Virginia 24251
   f. Noel, Missouri 64854
   (Inquire, these post offices - if you bundle your Christmas cards into a large envelope and address it to the postmaster in one of these towns, they postmark them and send the cards on their way.)

4. United States issued the first Christmas stamp in 1962.

5.   Many people abbreviate Christmas by writing *Xmas*. In Greek, x is the first letter of Christ's name. It was often used as a holy symbol.

6.   Wise old saying: Christmas is a holiday where neither past nor future is as interesting as the present.

7.   Bing Crosby's singing of *White Christmas* won an Oscar for best song in 1942 and turned into the highest selling record of all times.

8.   The poinsettia is a winter-blooming plant and must have fourteen continuous hours of darkness everyday for approximately seventy-six days in order to bloom at Christmas time.

9.   In the 1920's Santa Claus changed from black and white to color in ads for Coca-Cola.

10.   Prince Albert, a German, married his cousin Queen Victoria of England in 1837. He brought the Christmas tree custom to England.

11.   Mistletoe, thought by the Druids in early times to be holy, was considered to be a cure for poisons and was called "all heal".

12.   Superstitious people say holly tied to a bedpost will chase away nightmares. One

thing is certain, holly berries are poisonous and will certainly make you sick.

13. A Massachusetts law of 1659 fined anyone who was caught celebrating Christmas.

14. There are yearly Christmas season processions to Clement Clark Moore's grave in Trinity Cemetery in New York. Children sing carols and hear a recitation of his famous poem - *A Visit from Saint Nicholas* written in 1822.

15. *Rudolph, the Red Nosed Reindeer* was created in 1939 for Montgomery Ward and Company. It was after the Great Depression and they wanted something for the store Santa to hand to the children. This hand-out was a copy of the song.

16. First Christians were forbidden by the Roman government to practice their faith, so they worshipped secretly in caves called the Catacombs.

17. During the Middle Ages there was a legend that the Christ Child traveled through the night (Christmas Eve) looking for a place to stay. On Christmas Eve, families placed lighted candles in their windows as a welcome sign to the little "wanderer". On

that night, no stranger was turned away. The custom of placing candles in windows continues even today.

18. Kriss Kringle - gift-giver in the Dutch-English-German Pennsylvania placed gifts among branches of their Christmas tree instead of stockings.

19. In Greek and Orthodox churches, Christmas is celebrated January seventh since they follow the Gregorian calendar.

20. In Austria you seldom hear Christmas carols before December twenty-fourth. Advent songs are heard for the four weeks prior to Christmas.

21. The bagpipe is a favorite instrument used at Christmas in Italy.

22. Thomas Mast, famous cartoonist who helped translate Saint Nicholas to Santa Claus, also developed the symbols of the donkey for the Democratic party and the elephant for the Republican party.

23. The first trombones in America were brought by the Moravians. These instruments were used to announce all private and public occasions.

24. Theodore Roosevelt will be remembered for many things, not the least that of the teddy bear named for him and placed under Christmas trees for more than half a century.

25. Nicholas (later Saint Nicholas) was in attendance at the First Council of Nicene in 325 A.D. where the Nicene Creed was created.

26. The Pennsylvania Dutch farmers' trees were decorated only with home-made donuts and strings of dried apples.

27. Red, green, and white became Christmas colors because of several reasons. One was the early paradise tree which had red apples, white bread or wafers, and a green tree. Another was the Christmas holly which had green leaves and red berries found often in the white snow.

28. Ancient Romans held mass when the cock crowed around 3 A.M. in the morning.

29. In England and Canada they celebrate "Boxing Day". On this day boxes of presents are given to the poor as well as the mailman, newsboy, milkman, and all public servants.

30. Minnesota prides itself with having a lake in Scott County named Christmas.

31. We have five communities in the United States that have Christmas as their name:
    Christmas; Gila County, Arizona
    Christmas; Orange County, Florida
    Christmas; Lawrence County, Kentucky
    Christmas; Bolivar County, Mississippi
    Christmas; Roane County, Tennessee

32. February second is Candlemas on the church calendar. Candles are blessed. This commemorates the forty days after the birth of Jesus when Mary went to the temple to be purified. In those days this always had to be done by a woman who had a child.

33. Although Kriss Kringle has become popular as another name for our Santa Claus figure - in fact, it is a variant of the German for "Christ Child".

34. A superstition says: The weather on each of the twelve days of Christmas signifies what the weather will be on the appropriate month of the coming year.

35. On Christmas Eve 1870, during the Franco-Prussian War, the French and German troops were in nearby trenches. Suddenly one of the

Frenchmen jumped up and sang a beautiful solo song in honor of that evening. Adolphe Adam's "Cartique de Noel" (O Holy Night) was that solo. No Germans fired at him. Instead one of their soldiers merged and sang a German carol.

36. The wild boar, worshipped by the Druids in England and offered as a sacrifice to their goddess Frigga, symbolized the ploughing of the fields because of its tusks which dug into the earth. Since the time of Henry VIII, boars heads have been a part of many an English holiday meal.

37. Wassail "WAES-HAEL" was shouted by the Anglo Saxons as they toasted each other at holiday - time feasts. It meant "Be in good health".
A custom that developed in England, known as "Wassailing", in which villagers carried the brew door to door, drinking to the good health of their neighbors.

38. The Christmas cactus, which sends forth beautiful blossoms every year at Christmas time, is a native of Brazil. Here it grows on the branches and trunks of trees, similar to mistletoe. It is not, however, a parasite, but digs its roots into the moss and derives its moisture from the rain.

39. Mumming is difficult to define exactly since it includes every kind of dressing up and acting out or dancing or performing that people choose to do at Christmas time. It can be traced back to the time of Saturnalia when men dressed as animals or women, and caroused in the streets.

40. The term "Old Christmas Day" is still some times used in England for January 6, Epiphany.

THE OESTREICH'S TREES

PARADISE TREE OR ADAM/EVE TREE

The immediate ancestor of the Christmas tree was the paradise tree. We have Adam and Eve, the Biblical parents of the human race, to thank for the inclusion of the Christmas tree in the celebration of the birthday of our Savior. Up until the Middle Ages, the church had rejected the evergreen tree as a pagan tradition because the pagans considered it the symbol of eternal life. During the Middle Ages, however, the stories of the Bible were often acted out throughout the year by traveling players, who gave plays and pageants and other dramas for moral instruction. At that time the majority of the people were illiterate, meaning they could not read or write.

In the ancient liturgical calendar, the feast of Adam and Eve was celebrated on December twenty-fourth. Therefore, the "play of the day" for Christmas Eve was the story of Adam and Eve and how their fall into sin made clear the need of Christ's birth the next day. They called Christ the "second Adam" who redeemed the failure of the "first Adam".

These plays, done from Advent through Resurrection, were most often performed on the steps of the church; however, they became so popular that they also started to be performed in homes along with the setting up of the paradise tree.

A main set piece of this play was the paradise tree, a bare tree hung with apples, the tree from which Adam and Eve ate against God's command. It being winter, the tree used was a fir (evergreen) tree. The church fathers recognized that they could appease the people, who were eager to include trees in their Christmas celebration, and take advantage of the biblical story at the same time by tying together the story of the original creation and man's re-creation through the birth of Christ.

In keeping with the legend that trees bloomed when Christ was born, flowers were added to the tree representing life-everlasting through Christ. The apples represented man's fall into sin and the green tree (evergreen) stood for immortality. Finally wafers, as in communion wafers, were added as a symbol of the body of Christ and our salvation through Christ.

One of the trees in my home is the "Paradise Tree" also called the "Adam and Eve Tree" and "Tree of Life and Knowledge." On my tree I use sixty-six red apples representing the number of the books in the Bible. Thirty-three communion wafers, that I have gilded with gold and pin-holed with a tiny thread, stand for the years of Christ's life. Hanging on the tree is a long red serpent representing the devil and Adam and Eve glass-blown ornaments. I also stud the tree with dried flowers from the garden. This year I used hundreds of dried white annual statice.

ITALIAN CHRISTMAS TREE - THE CEPPO

The use of the evergreen tree is not a common custom in Italy. Their tree, shaped like a pyramid, is called a ceppo, meaning tree trunk. It is also called "The Tree of Light," the light being Jesus. The complete name is the Ceppo di Natale. The ceppo is a wooden frame with several tiers of shelves. On the shelves only religiously oriented items may be placed and at the ends of each shelf is a candle. Some of the items placed on the shelves in the early days were colored paper, cones, and candles. Under the ceppo the family would place the presepio, the Italian manger. This was the center of their Christmas celebration. The Bambino, the figure representing the Baby Jesus, was not put into the scene until Christmas Day being placed by the mother of the home. Many times a ceppo was built for each member of the family.

Our ceppo, of course shaped like a pyramid, is about six feet tall and is made of cherry wood. It has six shelves or tiers and is supported by the wooden frame. This was made by a good friend, Eugene Sears, from Woodville, Ohio.

Beneath our ceppo we place the presepio in which the Bambino is not placed until Christmas morning. The wisemen are added on Epiphany, January sixth.

On the first shelf we place the gold (precious valuable element), frankincense (fragrant resin) and myrrh (aromatic gum resin) because they were the gifts given to the Christ Child by the wisemen or Magi. Also on the shelf we place small, wrapped gifts representing our gifts to the ones we love.

On shelf two we have a complete communion set fashioned by friends from Swanton who are potters. Their business is the Harbor Hill Stone Crafts.

Three parts of the communion set are the flagon, the container that holds the wine; the paten, the flat dish that holds the wafer or unleavened bread; and the chalice, that holds the 'blessed' wine and may be used as the common cup for communion. As it says in Luke 22 : verses 14-22: "This is my blood, shed for you and this is my body broken for you."

Shelf three deals with God's creation of nature and is significant because of Saint Francis of Assisi an Italian who loved all forms of nature. On our shelf we have included a tree branch with a bird collection signifying Saint Francis. It also includes a single rose and a wheat sheaf. This then summarizes the plant and animal kingdom of God's creation. Genesis 1 discusses Earth's creation while Matthew 6: v. 31 says we should not be anxious for tomorrow for God will care for us. Then in Psalm 65 it says that God visits the earth with water and provides plants and animals for our use.

Shelf four holds a gothic cross, a lamb made of alabaster, the manger and Christ Child (until Christmas morning) and a rock relating to the stone that was rolled away on Easter morning.

Shelf five has the angel Gabriel, the angel that appeared to Mary in the sixth month.

> "Hail, O favored one, the Lord is with you! ... And behold, you will conceive in your womb and bear a son, and you shall call his name, Jesus."

Shelf six at the very pinnacle of the ceppo is a large white candle. White tends to be theological not Biblical. However, in Revelations 7: verses 13-14 it says:

> "Who are these clothed in white robes, and whence have they come? ... They have washed their robes and made them white in the blood of the Lamb."

Also woven throughout the ceppo are sprigs of holly since in the early days this was considered a holy plant.

Ceppo - Italian Christmas Tree

FRIENDSHIP TREE

This tree is a large seven foot tree that has ornaments from my family's life. On its branches hang ornaments made by my son, Brian and my daughter, Lisa. It has ornaments from trips Ruth, my wife, and I have taken. Ornaments given to us by our parents and many ornaments given to me when I taught school in Woodville, Ohio, are on the tree. Also many beautiful ornaments given to us by friends and individuals who have been on the Christmas tours hang as a symbol of love and friendship.

YUM - YUM TREE

This interesting tree is made of wood with a wooden dowl in the center and wooden branches that can be moved out in all directions. It is painted antique green and has candy hanging from and on the branches. It is a "welcome" type tree in which friends visiting can remove a piece of candy if they desire a treat. Vernon Wiersman, a friend made and gave me the tree when Ruth, Lisa, and I joined Saint John's Lutheran Church, Oak Harbor, Ohio.

TRADITIONAL GLASS ORNAMENT TREE

This tree is always a live - cut frazer fir. It is eight foot in height. The tree has 750 colored lights and 1075 (so far) glass ornaments, many of which are antique and have been passed down from generation to generation. We then use a loose artificial snow which gracefully lies on all the branches. Sometimes a garland is placed around the tree.

WALL TREE

Our wall tree is simply a flat one-sided evergreen tree that can be placed on a wall. It is decorated with small lights, garlands of tiny beads, and is studded with dried flowers like baby breath, roses, and annual statice. It is a great tree because it can be used year after year without removing the decorations. It is ideal for a small home, nursing home, or for someone who does not want to spend much time or energy in decorating.

POTPOURRI TREE

This tree was given to the family by a close friend named Liz Briggs. Again the tree may remain decorated year after year. It is constructed of a styrofoam cone, covered first with grapevine and then with Spanish moss. White miniature lights and dried flower garlands are then added with some ribbon or beads. The exposed areas of Spanish moss can then be sprayed with any kind of fragrance such as bay-berry, cinnamon, or vanilla. When the tiny lights get warm, the fragrance permeates the room. It is potpourri at its best because you do not have to bother with candles or hot water for permeation.

TWELVE DAYS OF CHRISTMAS TREE

We use a grapevine spiral wreath. Placed on it is ribbon and dried silver king, a wonderful perennial I grow in the garden. Hung from the decorated grapevine are the wooden, hand painted symbols from the carol, *The Twelve Days of Christmas*. They are: the partridge in the pear tree, two turtle doves, three french hens, four calling birds, five golden rings, six geese a-laying, seven swans a-swimming, eight maids a-milking, nine ladies dancing, ten lords a-leaping, eleven pipers piping and twelve drummers drumming.

CROWN TREE

The origin of this tree has been traced to Germany. The tree was then used in England when Prince Albert married Queen Victoria and they used the Christmas tree in their home. Other names for the tree are the "Inverted Tree" and "Ceiling Tree." The tree can be hung upside down, in others right side up but still suspended from the ceiling. The tree eventually made its way to America.

There are many stories of why this was done in this fashion. One story said that Prince Albert and Queen Victoria wanted a "different type" Christmas tree.

Others stories written say that some homes in early America were very tiny and room was scarce. By hanging the tree from the ceiling more room was available for the family. The children could also play under the tree. Since the tree ornaments were cookies, nuts, fruit and other goodies the children could not snatch them from the tree. Homes many times had rodents such on mice. With the tree suspended the edible ornaments were not as "available" to those creatures.

Our crown tree is hung upside down. It is a difficult tree to decorate because it is inverted. All garlands of ribbon, lace, and beads must be attached with tiny wires to keep them in place. Our tree has a Victorian decor because of its historical background relating to Queen Victoria. On it we use glass-blown ornaments and other Victorian styled ornaments in blue, silver, mauve, and white. The tree is "dressed" with white Christmas lights.

EARLY PIONEER DAY TREE

This tree uses candle holders and candles along with a garland of German pretzels, cookies, small loaves of dark bread, and other pastries. Also on the tree I use anything pioneers may have had in their home in those days. These items include many collectible cookie cutters, toys, wooden spoons, nut crackers, tin cups, shaving brushes, candy canes, children's blocks, apples and other fruit, nuts, chocolate molds, and home-made ornaments.

DRIED - FLOWER TREE

This tree has 750 miniature multi-colored lights along with 400 or more clusters of flowers that I have dried from my garden producing colors of red, white, purple, yellow, blue, orange, lavender, and pink. Each year there are at least thirty varieties of dried flowers that I use on the tree such as snapdragons, zinnias, annual and perennial statice, joe pye, silver king, gay feather, hydrangea, blackberry lily seed pods, bee balm, shasta daisy, yarrow, carnations, tansy, sweet annie, baby breath, lady's mantle, delphinium, columbines, and of course the beautiful roses which dry so easily. This tree is an extension of my summer garden and remains trimmed usually until March.

GOOSE - FEATHER TREE

Artificial feather trees continued to be sold in multitudes during the 1920's in U.S. because European born Americans were following a tradition done in their homeland. Many were sold by mail-order houses such as Sears Roebuck and Montgomery Ward.

Most feather tree manufacturing was a cottage industry, meaning it was done in a home setting. Most times the parts of the tree -- wire, wood, and berries -- were factory made. The heavy wire branches were sent to cottages for wrapping.

These trees were made by stripping the feathers off the quills after each feather was dyed. Then each heavy wire was individually wrapped with these green feathers. The feathers were carefully wrapped around and around the heavy wire, with the ends of each feather fastened with tiny thin wire. A new feather was fastened and thus the entire branch was circled by these green feathers. Each branch was finished at the end with either a berry or a candle holder. These branches were attached to the central wood pole which was then placed in a stand. The branches were directly inserted into the wood by means of a previously drilled or nail-punched hole with a bit of glue. The final touches consisted of painting the base and wrapping the pole to hide the bare wires.

They made the trees with sparse branches to resemble the white pine or fir trees which were native to the swamps of Germany. The spaces between the branches allowed the safe use of candles.

The earliest feather trees had round bases and sold for as much as a dollar. In the late 1920's feather trees started to appear in square bases. One large feather tree was offered for sale by Sears. It was eight feet tall, had 96 branches, with 148 smaller branches and sold for $8.98. This tree now would sell for several thousand dollars.

My goose-feather tree was brought to America by my grandfather over one hundred years ago. He was concerned that when he came to America there would be no fir trees to use at Christmas.

To adorn this tree I place German glass-blown ornaments like grape clusters, apples, churches, cottages, and even lady bugs and pickles. Also antique "kugels" and glass-bead garlands are used on this special and sentimental tree.

Refer to the section of this book entitled, Trimming the Christmas Tree (Ornaments) for a study of the ornaments that were traditionally used on the goose-feather tree.

Grandpa's Goose-Feather Tree

MEMORY TREE - MEMORY ROOM

One of our rooms is dedicated to the memory of our family's past. It centers around the memory tree in which we use white lights, a cranberry garland, and then cluster the tree with many photographs of the past such as the July fourth flood, the "Great Blizzard", parents, grandparents, friends, family, special occasions, trips, garden scenes, pets, holidays, etc.

Also in the room is a wall garland that holds all the pictures of special occasions from the past year.

Placed around the room are momentos such as baptismal outfits, professional books (my father was a funeral director), darts, graduation announcements, and parents' catechism books. The complete room means "Memory."

"FOR THE BEAUTY OF THE EARTH" TREE

> For the beauty of the earth,
> For the beauty of the skies,
> For the love which from our birth,
> Over and around us lie:
> Christ, our Lord, to you we raise
> This our sacrifice of praise.

Our *For the Beauty of the Earth* tree tries to convey the glory and beauty of everything that surrounds us. Used on the tree are gold Christmas lights and a garland of natural hemp rope. Also placed on the tree are dried flowers, ears of Indian corn, sprays of wheat and oats, sunflowers, teasels, cattails, flocked fruit, dried colored leaves, and angels, animals, and persons made of corn husks. Hung near the top of the tree is a scroll bearing the words of the above verse from *For the Beauty of the Earth*.

SPICE - HERB TREE

When you want an interesting aroma in a room at Christmas decorate a spice-herb tree. Our tree uses white globe-shaped lights along with a garland of "hops" (used in beer making). Many herbs and spices are placed on this tree such as dill, yarrow, fever few, spearmint, peppermint, basil, oregano, cinnamon sticks, etc. Some herbs and spices are simply placed on the tree while others are placed in netting, making interesting ornaments.

BELSNICKLE TREE

The German Belsnickle was one of the old world mythical spirits of Christmas who visited houses *just before* Christmas and gave the children toys or switches, depending upon their behavior in the past year. This also was practiced in Pennsylvania in Early America. Other names are given to Belsnickle depending upon the part of Germany. Some examples are Knect Rupprecht,

Servant Ruppert, or Pelznickle. Sometimes he has a very long beard, maybe floor length, and a fur coat that would be many sizes too big. Sometimes he wears a sheet and a mask. He is supposed to be Saint Nicholas' helper. If he gives you a bad report, there will be no presents from Saint Nick. Instead you may be given a switch or a lump of coal!

This was probably the German character that Clement Clark Moore had read about and caused him to say in his famous poem "dressed all in fur from his head to his foot."

Also Belsnickle was a devilish companion who accompanied Christkindl when she delivered presents to the children.

Now it is a custom for whole groups of children to dress up in costumes and go "Belsnickling," parading through the streets, to Christmas parties and friend's houses.

Linda Lindquist Baldwin in 1986 bought an Old Antique Santa Collections book at a garage sale for a nickel. She had a very strong interest and desire to own one of the authentic but costly paper mache Santas of the eighteenth and nineteenth century. Linda decided to create one for herself. She now re-creates the history of the Belsnickle, sculpting Santas all year. They can be found in collections across America and in Europe. Her creations are labeled as to the year they were designed.

All Belsnickles must have a Santa face on them. Some of my belsnickles are candy canes, bells, icicles, pine cones, trees, and snowballs.

Baldwin is also developing Snowsnickles in which all ornaments must have a snow covering.

My original ornaments were given to me as a Christmas gift from a good friend of my daughter, Liz Briggs.

CHILDREN'S TREE

Since our two children, Brian and Lisa , were babies we have had the children's tree also called "From Our House To Your House Tree." Each Christmas Santa Claus would bring each of the children a Christmas ornament that was appropriate for their age and interest. Brian's first ornament was a cupcake ornament because of his love for cake. Some of the other ornaments for Brian were Andy, a bicycle when he started to ride, a box of apples and a gallon jug labeled cider when he was top cider salesman in his Future Farmers of America cider sales, and a car when he started to drive.

A few of Lisa's ornaments were Annie, a milk can and cream can when she had the dairy goats, a bicycle, a car, and then all the Star Trek ornaments which she is continuing to collect.

When Brian moved he took his ornaments to his home to start his tree. This tradition is continuing and now the grandchildren also receive their ornament.

THE JESSE TREE

The Jesse tree is a symbol of Jesus' family tree. The tree with its symbols represent the Old Testament stories and events leading up to the birth of Christ. This is yet another interesting approach to the meaning of Christmas.

The use of this tree is based upon the prophecy of Isaiah 11: verses 1-2 : "and there shall come forth a rod out of the stem of Jesse, and a branch shall grow out of his roots, and the spirit of the Lord shall rest upon him."

The genealogy of Christ is frequently shown in the form of a tree which springs from Jesse, the father of David.

The Jesse tree symbols transform a Christmas tree into a "family tree" of Christ. Each ornament placed on the tree is the symbol of an ancestor of Christ or of a prophecy which foretells his coming.

The symbols are the sun, the tablets of the Law, the key of David, Bethlehem, the root of Jesse, Noah's ark, the Ark of the Covenant, the altar of holocaust, the apple, the Pascal Lamb, the pillar of fire, manna, the star of David, the Temple, the crown and the scepter, the sword of Judith, and the burning bush.

The sun represents Christ as bringing eternal life and light, and is based on the prophecy of Malachi: "But unto you that fear my name shall the Sun of righteousness arise with healing in his wings." The six-pointed Star of David symbolizes the lineage of Christ from the royal house of David. The burning bush symbolizes the Virgin Birth, and the prophecy of the birth is seen in the Bethlehem-emblem. The apple is a symbol of Christ, who took upon himself the burden of man's sin, and Jacob's ladder is interpreted as Christ reuniting mankind to God. The ladder has also been interpreted in a moral sense, with each of the fifteen rungs standing for a specific virtue. The lamb is one of the favorite, and most frequently used, symbols of Christ in all periods of Christian art. A typical reference is John 1: v. 29, The next day John sees Jesus coming unto him and says, "Behold the Lamb of God, which taketh away the sin of the world!" Noah's ark is a symbol of baptism, and Jonah in the whale symbolizes death and resurrection.

The stories of the Old Testament have been an unlimited source of inspiration for the visual arts. The burning bush was the subject of the triptych painted by Nicholas Froment in the thirteenth century. The star of David was a popular symbol in stained glass windows, as seen at the Cathedral of Lyons.

The Jesse Tree was an early form of design for the stained glass windows of great cathedrals, such as Chartres. In the portrayal of the descent of Christ from the line of David, there may be as few as four or five figures or as many as fifty. The twisting branches of the tree always start with Jesse and end at the top with Christ.

GERMAN BIRD TREE

Another tree we are going to have in Christmas 1998 is the German Bird Tree. The Germans considered birds to be a universal symbol of happiness and joy and considered it an absolute necessity to have them on the Christmas tree. Birds would be captured in the fall and placed in cages during the winter for entertaining the entire family. Today birds represent messengers of love.

Bird's nest ornaments are symbols of good luck. Legend has it that prosperity will come to any home that finds a bird's nest nestled among the branches of the family's Christmas tree.

On our 1998 tree will be birds, bird's nests, bird houses and possibly bird feeders. No glass blown ornaments will be used on this tree, only natural type ornaments. These are being purchased and made by friends and family. Also we are gathering small nests from the yards and woods of the area. Spanish moss nests will probably be used. The garlands will be natural such as popcorn or birdseed. Some of the bird houses will be made from wood taken from an old church that became my grandfather's barn and was used by my father and me as our milking barn when I was farming.

Now that we have searched into the sacred and secular aspects of Christmas, it is hoped that each reader will find more happiness and contentment for themselves and will be willing to share it with others around them.

May our hearts be over-flowing with peace, hope, love, joy, and generosity! Then let the excitement extend to everyone at Christmas and throughout the year.

ABOUT THE AUTHOR

Reed Oestreich was born and raised on a farm between Elliston and Graytown, Ohio. His parents were Melvin and Lillian (Miller) Oestreich. He has attended Graytown Elementary School, Oak Harbor High School, Bowling Green State University where he received his Bachelor's Degree in Elementary Education and his Master's Degree in School Administration.

Liking the elementary classroom he taught most of the thirty years in the fourth, fifth, and sixth grades in Woodville School which later became Woodmore Schools. He retired from the public school in 1990.

He is married to the former Ruth Reeder of near Genoa. They have two children Brian and Lisa. Brian and his wife Jan have two children Joseph and Benjamin.

At present Oestreich is an assistant at a local funeral home and joined the faculty at Bowling Green State University as a supervisor of student teachers.

He is very active at Saint John's Lutheran Church, Oak Harbor singing in the choir and working in the area of evangelism.

His hobbies are caring for his three and a half acre arboretum and garden, having garden tours, preparing and drying flowers, decorating his home for the Christmas season, and doing research on the subject of Christmas.

BIBLIOGRAPHY

Barth, Edna. *Holly, Reindeer, and Colored Lights*. New York: Houghten Mifflin Company, 1971.

Brenner, Robert. *Christmas Through the Ages*. Algler, Pennsylvania: Schiffer Publishing Ltd, 1993.

Cohen, David. *Christmas in America*. San Francisco: Collins Publishers, Inc., 1988.

Cole, Joanna. *A Gift From Saint Francis - The First Creche*. New York: Morrow Junior Book Company, 1989.

Cuyler, Margery. *The All Around Christmas Book*. New York: Holt, Reinhart, and Winston, 1982.

Del Re, Gerard and Patrica. *The Christmas Almanac*. New York: Doubleday and Company, Inc., 1979.

Duden, Jane. *Christmas*. New York: Crestwood House, 1990.

Giblin, James Cross. *The Truth About Santa Claus*. New York: Thomas Y. Crowell, 1985.

Goldsmith, Terrance. *Christmas Around the World*. New York: Robert Rogers House, 1978.

Jones, E. Willis. *The Santa Claus Book*. New York: Walker and Company, 1976.

Joseph, Robert. *The Christmas Book*. New York: Mc Afee Books for Lonenz Press, 1978.

Kennedy, Pamela. *A Christmas Celebration*. Nashville, Tennessee: Ideals Children's Books, 1992.

Lagerlof, Selma. *The Legend of the Christmas Rose*. New York: Holiday House, 1990.

Merck, Beth. *Christmas Ornament Legends*. Spokane, Washington: Old World Christmas, 1995.

Metcalfe, Edna. *The Trees of Christmas*. New York: Abingdon Press, 1969.

Penne, Restad D. *Christmas In America*. New York: Oxford University Press, 1995.

Ross, Corinne. *Christmas in Italy*. Lincoln, Illinois: Passport Books, 1991.

Snyder, Phillip V. *The Christmas Tree Book*. New York: Viking Press, 1976.

Stevens, Patricia Bunning. *Merry Christmas, A History of the Holiday*. New York: Mac Millan Publishing Company, Inc., 1979.

Stewart, Martha. *Martha Stewart's Christmas*. New York: Clarkson N. Potter, Inc., 1989.

Wernecke, Herbert. *Christmas Customs Around the World.* Louisville: Westminster Press.

-------. *Christmas in Austria.* Chicago, Illinois: World Book Encyclopedia, Inc., 1982.

-------. *Christmas In Colonial and Early America.* Chicago, Illinois: World Book Encyclopedia, Inc., 1975.

ABOUT THE COVER:

FRONT COVER

Dried Flower Tree

BACK COVER

Top Photo
Crown Tree

Left Middle Photo
Goose-Feather Tree

Right Middle Photo
Italian Christmas Tree
"The Ceppo"

Bottom Photo
Paradise Tree

Description of the trees found on pages 162-182.

TO ORDER WRITE OR CALL:

CreekSide Publishing Co.
1945 N. Oestreich Rd.
Graytown, Ohio 43432
(419) 862-3237